# AMERICA'S ENDLESS LOOP CRISIS

# AMERICA'S ENDLESS LOOP CRISIS

### ANGER AND TECHNOLOGY IN AMERICA

Worse Than The Watergate Crisis. Without Domestic Tranquility

# JAYSON REEVES

AND

## THE HURN FOUNDATION

# AMERICA'S ENDLESS LOOP CRISIS
## ANGER AND TECHNOLOGY IN AMERICA

iUniverse books may be ordered through booksellers or by contacting:

iUniverse
1663 Liberty Drive
Bloomington, IN 47403
www.iuniverse.com
1-800-Authors (1-800-288-4677)

Because of the dynamic nature of the Internet, any web addresses or links contained in this book may have changed since publication and may no longer be valid. The views expressed in this work are solely those of the author and do not necessarily reflect the views of the publisher, and the publisher hereby disclaims any responsibility for them.

Any people depicted in stock imagery provided by Thinkstock are models, and such images are being used for illustrative purposes only. Certain stock imagery © Thinkstock.

ISBN: 978-1-4917-9454-8 (sc)
ISBN: 978-1-4917-9453-1 (e)

Library of Congress Control Number: 2016905922

Print information available on the last page.

iUniverse rev. date: 05/05/2016

# TABLE OF CONTENTS

# INTRODUCTION

Observing the 1990s and approaching the year 2020 Anger and Technology in the United States has been part of "America's Endless Loop Crisis". Contrary to good American technology advancements "this" has been the sad, unlawful, and destructive course of Satellite and Computer systems causing an indecisive format of mental, physical, financial, and fatal harm. Then lately as Americans we occasionally suffer and recognize "unthinkable domestic and mass murders" as a severe Lack of Domestic Tranquility including a Lack of Prosperity that the Preamble of the United States Constitution grants to the American people. Understanding this, Endless anger, violence, fatal negligence, and financial conflicts or crime has been a tremendous concern within our changing times of technology in America.

These are the times of advanced satellites, computers, internet, wireless communication, and other device operating systems that intervene with the people whom are being effected to commit unthinkable crimes with bazaar or no logical motive. This concentration of technological products (c/o the commercial airspace and the people) have created a new atmosphere for needed and enforceable local, state, and federal regulation. These are vital concerns with different issues that are part of changing most industry and government standards of today to reduce the madness of various individuals committing crimes of mass murder, or domestic murder with occasional suicide, and or financial crimes. Then throughout America the vital question becomes "WHY" is so many people committing some of the worse violent acts in our history, and how do we solve this problem and crisis?

The People, Corporations, and Government in America along with some commercial satellite activity have consolidated a critical "Lack of Full Sovereignty" which outlines that overall we are moving backwards with a "loss of logical and vital Prosperity". As numerous corporations in America regularly put various technology to use or offer advanced products or services to customers – the people, and government have a duty to seek logical corrections to all unlawful or negligent issues of liability.

Understanding extensive and broad law court arguments there is 2 attorney's (contrary to Science & Engineering) that come to mind and that is Civil Rights attorney Thurgood Marshall (also a former Supreme Court member), and attorney Archibald Cox (Special Prosecutor for the Watergate Trails). This is due to the magnitude of cases they argued, apart from the devastation of Charles Manson, and Jim Jones. Also other professionals such as computer programmers, computer analyst, satellite programmers, lawyers, engineers, scientist, and others who recognize scientific principals and even artificial intelligence whom must argue to the extent of administrative law judges that the individual state Constitution's, and the U.S. Constitution needs enforcement to correct this Endless Loop. This is vital at levels of resources that create a balance of American Constitutional Laws that apply to bad or unlawful use of satellites and other "technology".

The format of legal arguments in America consist of steps and actions that are only part of the problematic applications of today's technology and commercial airspace that has more so increased the level of anger that a tremendous amount of people have displayed. As Bill Gates and Paul Allen created Microsoft software this was established to better manage a "computer disk operating system" to organize computer programs, and files as them, NASA and others did not really establish these systems to destroy innocent people with violent conflicts or crime. Then as computers, satellites, and other devices within networks came together in a lawful and diversified capacity this slowly became a tool of crime for some people as this is one of the U.S. government's oversight issues of technology concerns. Otherwise the use of commercial satellites and certain networking technology (computers, cell phones, TV's, & radio) has overruled some values of common knowledge in our American society with some factors of anger and violence consisting of unexplainable motives with destruction, and unthinkable crimes.

The author Jayson Reeves has written this book to try and give the American general public his trials, experiences, professional knowledge, research, and slight arguments on these subjects of anger and technology. This is the lawful passion to inform the citizens of the United States, the American system of government, and others about this mental, physical, financial, and fatal crisis. Once we as a developing nation and society of restructured values are clear about the revisions and legislative corrections to reduce or eradicate technology that instigates destructive anger, financial disasters, fatal explosions, extreme violence, and other issues -- we more than likely will become a well-developed nation of operational solitude, prosperity, and domestic tranquility again.

# HOW ANGER & TECHNOLOGY COLLABORATED
## (1)

# CHAPTER ONE
## (1)

Anger and Technology In America

Worse Than The Watergate Crisis, Without Domestic Tranquility

# HOW ANGER & TECHNOLOGY COLLABORATED

(1)

The American society has numerous issues of anger and technology that have collaborated a resource of good, bad, and diversified concerns into complex conditions. This clearly has been a concern for the past (c/o the 1950s), and future between the years of 1990 to 2020. Conditionally this consist of almost, everyplace where Americans peacefully gather. Therefore as we have observed issues during the 1990s and 2000s massive harm becomes potentially dangerous environmentally and socially in most all safely considered parts of America. Then the concept of financial matters, marital conflicts, manufacturing explosions, other issues, and more so anger with violence has even more so become a tremendous Endless Loop Crisis.

These issues of anger and massive violence has been displayed in places like schools, church's, theater's, shopping malls, household's, and numerous other places. Then these issues will require that the people, and government evaluate, understand, and determine a solution along with good, and bad issues of National Security outlined in the United States and recently other well developed countries. Otherwise some of these factors became the benchmark of direction within good, and more so bad satellite technology that can occasionally, and conditionally cause harm, or even instigate destructive anger.

Another concern includes providing solutions for "most conflicts during" the recent, and consistent level of "Anger and Technology" throughout America. Observing good, and bad activities in America has lately been inconsistent with our United States Constitution's "Domestic Tranquility", as this creates tremendous problems. Therefore these become conditions of mental, physical, financial, and fatal disasters as the American system of government is not providing a lawful, and logical government solution too -- "fast enough" to save people. Understanding this, numerous Americans are then becoming more prone to anger, and violence without logical or clear motives. This consideration of issues could, and has been part of the worse level of "cyber or satellite" attacks against American citizens in history.

As it applies to certain solutions for satellite violations of law, and or cyber attack's two governed goals on occasion becomes -- logical confidentiality, and affirmations that is mentioned in the 4th Amendment of the U.S. Constitution -- that states "The right of the People is to be secure in their persons, houses, papers, and effects against unreasonable searches and seizures, shall not be violated, and no warrant shall issue, but upon probable cause, supported by oath or affirmation, and particularly describing the place to be searched, and the person or things to be seized". Understanding these goals would also reduce all illegal U.S. domestic, and international spy's. This sometimes may include or exist from diversified foreign nationality owned television, and radio stations which includes other American conflicts. Also this would include the lawful, and not unlawful expansion of wired and wireless phone companies of a logical capacity. This valued concern can include unreasonable searches (c/o commercial satellites) that is part of obtaining information illegally, contrary to knowing whom is being informed to use negative and unlawful technology as a conflict of interest.

As we understand "immigrates and Americans" recently, the 1st and 4th Amendments of the U.S. Constitution has been occasionally part of violations and terrorizing people by instigating them into numerous law infractions. These are tremendous violations of law, and conflict that constantly cost money, time, and logical reputation. Observing this, the valuable factor of Domestic Tranquility that the Preamble of the U.S. Constitution mentions, and acknowledges as important is vital to social resources of stability. Then this understanding becomes relevant as Americas religious freedom is not to become a threatening or manipulating factor similar to some religious terrorist regions of the Middle East causing a strong lack of domestic tranquility. Basically domestic tranquility was established for how we should live safely in a productive, and morally prosperous way in America. Then our actions must go along with these "Constitutional" words of this central factor of law or even the doctoring of those like the Reverend Martin Luther King.

The observation of another factual concern is the 1st Amendment Rights of Religion, and Free Speech as arbitrary social media on the internet has occasionally achieved conflicting concerns. Then the Constitutions fairness to all people over the logic of this lawful discipline has been an unlawful attempt and an achievement of worded or explicit bulling. Also the concept of the internet's social media has been important technology, but it also has levels of concern for regulation and needed Constitutional amendments. These are concerns of occasional Unrestricted Free Speech that becomes harmfully destructive along with some conflicts of social and religious intimidation -- similar to overall diversified satellite and internet bullies.

The 1$^{st}$ Amendment and Domestic Tranquility issues today (c/o 2014) which includes an Endless Loop Crisis must be considered from the lowest to the highest courts, and most vital legislative branches of government in America. This has been an important concern due to some of our most diversified losses, and some of the worse tragedy's in U.S. history. Understanding this observation, Americans have good days, and bad days with issues that must be corrected by the people along with the courts, and the overall system of government. Then these laws with regulation will include professional engineering which interacts with professions like "computer and satellite programming" creating various other advanced technology disciplines of socially good values. Therefore most U.S. Congressional or legislative concerns with numerous state or local government values must maintain support for Americas resource of technology to produce lawful stability for the people.

Evaluating a comparison of losses which consist of the $11 trillion dollars of wealth that vanished from millions of American households approaching the years of 2006, and 2007 has been tremendous with severe anger, and tremendous dissatisfaction. Then contrary to economics, also before, during, and after the same time -- tens of thousands of children, and adults were killed in discretionary murders, domestic murder, or mass murders which include occasional suicide. Considering these factors of tremendous dissatisfaction, violence, and harm observed by citizens, numerous professionals, and government officials have recognized these diversified tragedies with concern for legislative corrections. Then their only emotions consisted of sadness, madness, anger, and some conflicting grief with no logical solutions for these suspects, and or defendants with their tragic or conflicting motives.

Observing these, and other tragic acts within violence as it applies to doctors of internal medicine a Washington D.C. physician Dr. Janis Orlowski outlined "in 2013" how sad, and rapid these violent tragedies are becoming. Considering her statement after a Washington D.C. naval yard fatal shooting like all logical American doctors consisted of how other professionals are to think, and live by professional standards as she acknowledged that the blood shed has taken a tremendous toll. Issues such as these have been tragic for her and other medical professionals to treat these victims of all ages from mass murder or with severe injuries from discretionary, and uncalled for anger which became severely violent.

The concept of domestic murder with occasional suicide has occurred with factual observation in Dr. Orlowiski's hospital physician residency, and other regional hospitals around America at record rates. If the suspected defendant lives, most cases when technology is a provoking or instigated factor, the courts still have not consisted of a detailed court argument within proceedings. Therefore the continuous concept of financial, and violent crimes has taken a toll on a massive amount of people, and a concerned amount of professionals, including citizens throughout the American society.

With a high rate of infant mortality (c/o 2007), and over the decade a low rate of marriages between "men and woman" the American society has been part of an unstable issue of corrections for a better social establishment. These are issues that must be properly corrected apart from continued "self or social destruction". This becomes the fact that even babies and children are born innocent, and most times they have no ability to control their lives contrary to marriage and or child care. Therefore the diversified issue of themselves, and or the conditions that they must live through are part of an occasional conflicting society. Considering this, even observing violence, terrorism, and economic conflicts these issues have somewhat been worse for a broad concentration of Americans.

As a comparison of the Great Depression (c/o the 1930s) upon which the American society has suffered from recently, is now an evaluation concern similar to the array of crisis conditions of pass public, private business, and government legislative values. This is a concern which has been part of compounded laws that were repealed or ignored with no valid legal court argument or discipline. Then this is the observation of how technology has changed in the millennium years of 2000 compared to laws that were ignored and created in the 1950s up to the years of 2000 plus. Understanding this the American society will only improve if the leadership within government, certain corporations, and most individuals appropriate, and mandate this awareness and the right changes within state and federal laws.

Understanding various disastrous issues of anger, violence, and technology; the question of why is so much conflicting madness with mental, physical, financial, and fatal harm becoming a reoccurring problem? This is not just a social and technology mystery, but clearly problems that require long term and resourceful solutions. Also this has been worse than any historical time in America, besides our centuries of conflict and indifference.

The pass century old factors of indifferent values consisted of black people in slavery, civil rights struggles, disease out brakes before mandatory vaccinations, a holocaust in Germany (c/o Jews moving to America) then international terrorism, and wars involving millions of Americans. Contrary to recent "international investments and international terrorism" lately these are issues which must be corrected. Then this becomes the logic of corrections that the American system of government, and the people must evaluate or find a solution for within all the people to have and maintain domestic tranquility with logical progressive prosperity.

Observing governed reliability due to more networking technology that is sometimes disturbing the American society has occasionally been a losing factor of reliability, and dependable social disciplines. This issue of reliability is part of the Domestic Tranquility, and all Prosperity that the United States Constitution "Grants to the People, Limits to the People, and Protects the People Against any Abuse" that applies to this central factor of law. More so this has recently included the factor of new technology without lawful, and logical enforcement to understand and enforce new technology resources. Then the consideration of Americans whom will destroy each other, numerous innocent citizens, and or various public/private or government assets has increased to dangerous levels.

Contrary to Americas recent war in the Middle East; children in the United States with or sometimes without parents have a requirement of money, education, food, clothing, and other necessities in order to live. This being one of the worse war time economies in the United States, it's important to survive in a productive way. Then this becomes making domestic tranquility a vital part of this American equation of importance. As "Domestic Tranquility" is outlined in the Preamble of the United States Constitution; the 14th Amendment "Prohibits all levels of government from denying to any person the equal protection of the laws". This goes along the fact that lawyers may, or may not argue a law case right, and then the U.S. Constitution with other laws are not truly livable documents which has more so supported an enemy foreign agenda of terrorism. Therefore its complex to explain that inappropriate discrimination should not overrule the Constitution's preamble, all other parts of Constitutionally applied laws, and "Prosperity" for the people.

With newly advanced technology the American system of government along with the courts have work to provide regulatory values to every lawful concern for "legally established domestic tranquility". This is what makes domestic tranquility, and prosperity an established livelihood throughout the American society that is "now" in need of vital corrections. These are some of the protections granted by the Constitution of the United States for various assets, workable occupations, religious standards, various professions, educational disciplines, and regulatory standards with concern for all American citizens.

Understanding anger and technology in America during the 1990s, and the first decade of 2000 has shown us mental, physical, financial, and fatal crimes and occasional negligence as this has been a time of historic crisis. These crisis conditions also consist of severe negligence that is destroying parts of America slowly at conflicting record rates. Although very few issues of prosecution over technology laws have occurred with consistent circumstantial evidence, historical or political facts, and scientific principals has been more of a judicial review crisis. Then a tremendous consideration of unattended scientific principals that can cause unenforceable destructive activities apart from laws has pushed America backwards. Otherwise this concern which sometimes ended in some form of a crisis, and with ineffective court hearings has continued to get worse.

My evaluation during the 1990s and 2000s has caused a percentage of various disastrous matters to be "an Endless Loop Crisis" that must be corrected through the courts, and the American system of legislature. This has been a critical concern throughout Indiana, Illinois, Ohio, Michigan, Arizona, and even the surroundings of Washington D.C. including other state matters like in New York. Contrary to these facts most lawyers have not, or are not willing to argue these cases in a preventative factor of collaborated discipline, but some will violate these complex laws which are extremely complex to prosecute, and or argue. Therefore "protecting victims" even as it applies to terrorist living inside, and or outside of America has been observed at a critically low, but concerned rate until after September 11, 2001.

Another Endless Loop Crisis "vital" factor is the Illegal and Hazardous Commercial Satellite use that is destructively active in America which massive amounts of people vaguely understand. This is a severe, and massive problem with numerous laws that exist, and with the need for new artificial intelligent legislature (c/o satellites and other complex enforceable technology) to be passed into law. Then with enforcement applicable to regulation with logical affirmation's needed, the future can consist of more responsible social standards of living. These issues are valued within the use of certain technological equipment being used against the American people, or the United States overall.

Observing an Endless Loop Crisis whether as an international or domestic crime, spy's, or occasional industry negligence which occurs, some resources of technology and communications are vital to lawfully enforce and legislatively correct. These are technology issues such as from television, radio, satellite radio, satellite imagery certain phone companies, and other technology that become a "broad" factor of concern. Then these factors have been vital issues creating a gap between people that are rich, poor, good, and or bad individuals. With this understanding the U.S. economy has become an issue where a vast amount of Americans can't prosper or advance financially. Observing this, the United States Constitutional laws that apply to technology must be reviewed, and enforced with the peoples affirmed understanding of a well-developed society, a concentration of good and bad technology, and how to improve bad technology values of a prosperous society.

Understanding "Affirmation" which is outlined in the 4th Amendment of the U.S. Constitution various active technology having a sociological effect such as with Commercial Satellite operations throughout the American airspace can be critically inadmissible with no affirmation and dangerous. This vital issue of inadmissibility with very little affirmed evidence in a court of law is making lawful (satellite) Affirmations slightly "non-existent" and disastrous to certain innocent people of our American society. Therefore any business or company like television and radio stations, and various other industries with access to the airways or airspace must have legal authenticated station identification, code affirmations, and other reported details. Then this includes broadcast names, having a registered broadcasting license, or statement of authorized use permits which is affirmed with the appropriate communication agencies, and government authorities.

The internet with satellite issues can be more admissible in the courts with affirmations, but inadmissible satellite use upon acting as a spy, or spying on other local citizens, or diversified business owners is a more severe, and complex subject even effecting various tax base values. This is a problem of inadmissible affirmation which has reached an all-time low, and crisis within safe or lawful satellite technology use and "protective business values of existence". Then therefore our American society should recognize that the Federal Communication Commission (FCC), and the Federal Trade Commission (FTC) along with various other state and federal agencies including most Constitutional laws as being vital to be astute, enforced, and active.

Having an observation of accessible "Satellite" companies, Computer companies, Computer component companies, and "Wireless" communication companies consist of regulated technology standards. The format of these regulatory values are, or must be technical, and slightly uniformed laws which become vital in these rapidly changing times of industry and more so technology. These are diversified businesses like Comcast, *Oracle Corporation, Dish Network Corporation, Microsoft Corporation, Google, Apple Inc., AT&T (c/o Ameritech Crop), Verizon, News Corporation, Echostar Communication Corp, General Electric Corp, MCI-WorldCom, a few others, and those connected to Landsat. Observing Landsat is one of the more complex satellite entities, they have went from being a government operation to being controlled by public and or private businesses. Then we must observe, and know that government is maintaining these and various overall regulatory duties with discipline.

As a vast amount of other companies consist of (foreign and U.S. domestic) television, and radio stations (c/o licensing) their use and liability of commercial satellites for radio, television, and other media values has been extremely good, bad, and severely conflicting. Observing this, there are more companies, and people more than ever with access to "wireless and satellite technology" that must comply with the American government's system of regulation. Then this is the understanding that a creative "but lawful" level of regulation must be applied to America's lawful conditions of livable standards for everyone to maintain a prosperous life, which vitally includes domestic tranquility.

A variation of companies that survived, and then failed differently were News of The World, Enron Corporation, and WorldCom Corporation along with the inadequacy of Ameritech Corporation and a few other communication companies. An even more greater responsibility is that these corporate, and or other types of businesses are required to comply with various regulative issues of law with standard disciplines of responsibility. These are "safety, confidentiality, economic, communication, or other business or social regulative standards" which also includes the 4th Amendment with other law disciplines. This then vitally is part of the input and output of all standard operations of the internet, satellites, and telecommunication companies which therefore has legal oversight technology concerns.

The concept of failure within businesses occasionally is the result of very serious crimes, or a conflict of "negative interest, human error, bad technology, and other conflicting resources". Observing this, these concerns which sometimes consist of horrific violence or crimes for money, power, or other concerns are part of issues that have more than likely consisted of instigated or provoked murder and disasters. Then "conditionally" with no Affirmation (c/o satellites) observing the courts in a majority of the time, numerous Court of Law Case Reviews in a "murder suicide" judicial format have very little or "nothing to argue" in the courts. Some of these become law cases that can not be easily proven with a solution (c/o that all involved are dead), apart from any corrections, punishment, or even to provide any compensation is an issue that may become extremely complex or important to resolve.

This book – America's Endless Loop Crisis (co Anger and Technology in America) by the author Jayson Reeves will outline a few major issues that have seem to lead to mass murder, domestic household murders, and or economic household destruction. The concept of this is factual within the American mortgage crisis, the bubble busting dot Com era, and the economic recession during the 1$^{st}$ decade of 2000. These also are issues that may have resulted in the 1999 Columbine High School shooting, the 2006 Pennsylvania Amish school shooting, the 2007 Virginia Tech massacre, the 2012 Sandy Hook Elementary School shooting, the 2013 U.S. Naval Yard shooting in Washington D.C. near Rhode Island, and the 2012 Aurora, Colorado movie theater shooting with various other violent domestic murders, and financial crimes at a large capacity.

Observing various crisis concerns, there were other disasters within "misunderstood" societal and household acts of violence, financial fraud, and other crimes in America that have devastated numerous communities. These are acts which have stunned our valued society of laws, and technology as a well developed nation. Considering this, anger and dissolution in America to correct various matters has only increased to critical levels. Then apart from the massive work needed by the people and government the review of good, and bad technology with government and social concerns of study have become vital for the right executive, legislative, and judicial government solutions.

As recent tragedies like the 2 massive shootings at the U.S. military base of Fort Hood in Texas, these acts have given the American society extreme worries about various issues. These issues linger with discretionary motives for this level of violence. This level of anger in the U.S. Department of

Defense on various military bases in America has been accompanied by suicide, rape, murder, homosexuality, domestic violence, fatal negligence, and other conflicts. Then with other violence upon which this holds, is a severe level of occasional instability. The level of instability means ill moral livable standards.

The 2009 fatal shooting at Fort Hood was by (officer) Nidal Hasan whom wounded 30 people, and left 13 other American people dead. Then in 2014 (specialist) Ivan Lopez killed 3 people including himself, and wounded 13 other American solder's. Therefore this leaves the American society, and government with the fact that something radical including technology has become a vital problem. This understanding is vital within social standards of how we must try to live in a society of domestic tranquility, but this is Non-Domestic Tranquility.

Considering the numerous law cases of domestic murder with occasional suicide, American's have been plagued with conflict in the United States that is unprecedented. This has been enormous throughout Indiana, Illinois, Arizona, Colorado, Oklahoma, Texas, and various other states near the capital of Washington D.C., including its surrounding metropolitan areas. Most of these violent acts, and law cases are different contrary to the 1995 bombing destruction that Timothy McVeigh, and Terry Nichols caused to the people in the "Oklahoma" Alfred P Murrah federal building. This disaster seem to be one of the major starting points of an Endless Loop Crisis of internal destruction on American soil. Otherwise economic, and social disasters with other conflicts including the terrible Oklahoma City bombing was fairly part of an unconscious act similar to countries that are becoming undeveloped, but all the same this was an extremely destructive issue of non-tranquil conflicting anger.

One enormous argument recently has been the 2nd Amendment of the United States Constitution which is the Right to Keep and Bear Arms, and issues of gun control. Considering this, it takes a human to pull the trigger of a gun to be harmful. My belief in this book is that some motives were instigated by various people, and issues of satellite technology apart from gang violence, and other conflicts. This becomes a major diversion between guns, satellites, people, and various Constitutional law disciplines.

Occasionally the concept of someone being mentally coerced by instigated or manipulated conflict becomes a vitally mad concern. These issues of concern on occasion are a diversified result of Illegal and Hazardous Commercial Satellite use instigating the conflicts of gun use or other violence which can create tragic results. This then becomes no different than gang members instigating or provoking violence against any other rival or their own gang members, and or assets of various other citizens. Understanding the unlawful satellite issue becomes the conflicting, and more so "complex" resources of evidence when Americans suffer. Then this becomes the highly inadmissible evidence within someone hearing voices (contrary to violent gangs or people), as these people "can- not" control certain distractions easily in the commercial airspace.

Illegal and Hazardous Commercial Satellite use which applies to people hearing voices was my partial case review, and observation of Aaron Alexis, the 34 year old 2013 shooter that killed 12 people at a Washington D.C. Navy Yard. Observing him and an enormous amount of other people, he made statements of hearing "voices". This factor was consistent with so many other Americans committing these or conflicting tragic acts of violence. Contrary to the circumstances of these people like Aaron Alexis hearing voices, they have to talk about it, recognize who's voices are being heard, and then the most complex issue of how to make it stop through logical resources of government. Therefore one major issue of people hearing voices is that internal medicine has rarely or ever worked to solve this problem completely, but government should recognize the clear root of this technological problem and crisis.

Considering a vast amount of people including Aaron Alexis that more than likely are effected by Illegal and Hazardous Commercial Satellite use this is a problem they "can not" solve by themselves. This is similar to someone intentionally trying to lock someone into a gas chamber or more so a "communication spectrum chamber" with mental madness increasing. Therefore he and others were hearing voices they could not eliminate, stop, or ignore during these terrorizing issues of conflict. Then this conflict has become a common problem, and crisis for thousands of Americans which must be corrected through somewhat medicine and more so technology regulation that is properly enforced by government.

The diversified force of laser technology, satellite technology, and a few other product resources with liability for authorized (c/o government) uses have occasionally failed with bad users throughout the American society. Considering good, and bad technology the misconception of secured technology include the fact that none of these resources, and or government officials prevented people from being victimized in the World Trade Center's on 9-11-2001. Observing this terrorist attack these American people were victimized to the point that they could not survive, or stop these massive buildings from crushing them to death. Understanding this,

American technology which includes numerous people (c/o even National Security and the Central Intelligence Agency) did not serve, and protect these American assets, and people on September 11, 2001.

Observing lasers, and satellites causing people to be victims, and then defendants (contrary to terrorist) is part of very complex technological systems. Some officials, or conflicting people say it is to protect patents or the American people and society of the United States. Contrary to this, the use of this equipment has been out of control, and "like machinery" not easy or impossible for normal people to cut off. Also it becomes complex to regulate, and or be used with total safety, and lawful disciplines of the innocence of American people. Then having Constitutional "Total Silence", and "Total Confidentiality" (c/o "hearing voices" or "being heard") in the commercial, and or residential Airspace with Logical Affirmations has become a tremendous, and a complex crisis for many families.

The people unlawfully using satellites apart from lasers "upon which they" are occasionally just as bad as terrorist, consist of various types of people acting like dictators. This includes anybody employed with the American system of government considering a victim/defendant (c/o the people) consistently or most times may not recognize a voice with no lawful affirmation. Another similar, and technical silent killer of comparison is the enclosed effect of carbon dioxide as a silent or invisible killer. This is a chemical that is occasionally impossible to see, and quite hard to detect besides a deadly or the impartially slight odder of gas. Understanding this, certain issues of detection apply with vital observation and active corrections that are important for human survival. Therefore we can only slightly recognize regulatory improvements for lasers, satellites, and gases like carbon dioxide which can be highly fatal, and or dangerous without careful, and responsible use.

Contrary to hearing voices a vast amount of violent domestic gun crimes have been committed, and have ended some families existence. This issue becomes more complex then gang violence, and the lawful or unlawful use of anything considered a weapon including drowns, cars, satellites, knives, a gun, and or even the ownership of a gun with a regulated permit. Then understanding this, the vital review of the judiciary, and certain legislative issues of amended laws with government adjustments must be actively established for logical enforcement. Considering this, these legislative amendments apply to issues like new technology that may cause an extensive amount of unpredicted anger, deaths, or even fatal or nonfatal violence.

Observing the people of the United States during 2007 an enormous amount of Americans loss their homes, retirement savings, and even their jobs as businesses suffered conflicts. This was part of an economy that affected a vast amount of American people upon which the United States government established the Troubled Asset Relief Program (TARP) that has consisted of economic losses to be somewhere around $11 trillion dollars. As this applies to technology some financial crimes surrounding the use of commercial satellites, and networking computers (c/o even cell phones) has been an occasional element of concern. Therefore apart from lawfully helpful technology product use, these issues sometimes force people to make bad, or negligent decisions which becomes an aggressive conflict within the American society we live in to recover from.

Another major government concern and conflict has been the Glass Steagall Act which was repealed through the U.S. government. This legal resource of legislature gave banks more money and control to compete, or operate against investment banks. Also the Glass Steagall Act along with mostly TARP funding was used to "save" too big to fail businesses, and banks with massive amounts of employees. Understanding this, extensive loans to citizens that failed with complex assets, bad professional decisions, and or certain activities surrounding crime consisted of some investments which have destroyed some peoples retirement, and or their lives. Then these financial issues connected to most banks in America has caused an economic recession which was the partial, and disastrous result of this Glass Steagall Act repeal.

As other technology issues had been adjusted with more high speed computers, and advanced technology, complex crimes were committed with unproductive disruptions to logical American business. This was observed within "land based, and or some orbital satellites". These issues "of deceptive use" became some of most destructive social standards in American history. Observing this, the American system of government was pressed to find solutions that are consistent with the U.S. Constitution as these technology issues have been out of control. Then considering these facts the U.S. Constitution is in need of an Amendment that regulates computers, satellites, or even technology similar to the U.S. Constitution on guns, and alcohol.

The 2007 economic conditions, and financial issues in America are strongly compared to the 1920s Great Depression which was disastrous with some people who did harm themselves. Also other people of that economic despair had to live in the most extremely bad parts of society. As times have changed with laws, and economic support from the American system of government, the people have found some improved economic values of survival. Therefore even with inflation and other issues of occurrence there is still an endless pressure point in various matters that must be considered in the solutions to these problems. Then as some laws go back 70 to 100 years or longer the American system of government must be careful about the reputation and enforcement of the changing times of "scientific principals and technology" concerning numerous laws throughout the American society. This is vital for most critically established laws to not be overlooked, or then they may destroy people, and or various parts of the American society with destructive attributes.

As the professions of law, engineering, accounting, and others (contrary to governments relationship with law professionals) lately the consideration of a person's pass crimes has been instigated as part of conditional problems, or concerns. Contrary to this fact a vast amount of the most violent mass murders occasionally was committed as some peoples first serious crime. Understanding all people must learn the laws, contrary to people making mistakes upon maturity, defamation, bullying, or acknowledgment with the consideration of a criminal record, only certain values can be observed besides the loss of life that can't be restructured. These values are within forgiveness, and opportunity, apart from persecution which are some of the principals that can create a more Perfect Union, Domestic Tranquility, and Prosperity for more American people in the United States are and should be under consideration.

In various concerns of life there are normal conflicts, instigated disputes, and manipulated or crimes committed by certain people sometimes having criminal records. This logic of a criminal record has not always been a solution for destructive results or opinions. Contrary to the fact, occasionally this is a discrepancy, or it becomes a more factual concept of effective government, and business which includes ambitious employment opportunities without crime of complacent conflicts. Then this not being the best equal opportunity part of most all answers within productive employment valued social standards as some American employers have ignored good productive citizenship values. This therefore has allowed more foreign people "good and bad" access, and financial support to occasionally destroy (c/o some mistakes) numerous American public, private business, or government valued assets with life-long citizens frustrated.

Considering diversified frustration it is true that some criminals will never change with the concept of offering forgiveness, and or with reconstructive living as this becomes part of moral, and vital determination. Also this includes people that violate laws in reference to executive orders or court martial offences. These severe violations of law can go on for long periods of time without prosecution for certain citizens or government officials, and this usually causes tremendous suffering. Apart from severe suffering this then even becomes disturbing attitudes for other crimes, if not the worse concept of violence.

Understanding conflicting crime and the Statute of Limitations (Liability Act) can be occasionally observed as inadequate due to lawyers that don't argue complex cases. This is the concern that even some lawyers and other professionals that violate these laws along with some government officials have continued to ignore, make excuses, and deny peoples 5th Amendment Due Process of Law rights. These actions are by certain American Bar Association members (c/o bad attorneys) with other conflicting professionals, or government officials. Then this includes certain judges and victims that go without lawfully supportive prosecution, or legal action which most citizens "can not" afford. Therefore justice becomes an unequal balance of events with unlawful conflicts that may continue to occur.

Most cities and towns in America observe values within the effort to maintain good domestic tranquility, and the prosperity of our American society. Then even as some foreign people migrate to the United States for employment, a vast amount of Americans will not be respected for their commitment to employment, and professionalism after some concerns of a questionable criminal past. These become strong factors of vital humanitarian concerns which now (c/o some past issues) that critically exist in America. Therefore this is a vital problem in a society that values the United States Constitution without abuse, unreliable opportunities, and especially as it may apply to the 5th Amendment.

Observing the 5th Amendment of the U.S. Constitution, "Due Process of Law" which resides under the Rights in Criminal Cases are lawful values to live by apart from being a victim or defendant in the courts. This becomes important as all people are to be fairly treated equal, even after being convicted of a crime and or when "just compensation" is ordered by a court becomes vital. The issue of compensation is conditional apart from the many prosecutors, politicians, and others near Corporate America that will sometimes hide or support these destructive people. Understanding these issues is part of the "American Justice System" that must be pursued with aggressive discipline, considering a sense of logic with ethical values, and lawful action. Then observing this to make government, and the judiciary recognize critical or destructive issues of law, scientific-principals, and the enforcement of legislative matters becomes vitally relevant to our future years of anger, technology, and domestic tranquility for the people

# ANGER IN AMERICA

(2)

## CHAPTER TWO

(2)

Anger and Technology In America

Worse Than The Watergate Crisis, Without Domestic Tranquility

# ANGER IN AMERICA

(2)

During the last decade of 1990, and the 1ˢᵗ two decades of the millennium years of 2000 America has observed tremendous anger, violence, certain economic conflicts, and various tragic issues concerning technology. Understanding this outburst of anger, it has went from gang violence, violent school shootings, shootings with fights in department stores during Christmas, shootings in church, domestic household murder with occasional suicide, and the list goes on and on. Even international, and U.S. domestic acts of massive destruction like various bombings, the major airline hi-jacking (9-11-2001), and various issues of aiding a foreign enemy have been occasionally worse than any historical time in America.

The concept of anger in America has truly become complex with the factual 9-11 Report terrorist attacks, the Oklahoma City bombing in 1995, and a massive amount of people killed in other places have been consistent tragedies with sometimes no logical, or clear to understand motives. This level of anger has become a rational concern that the American system of government is only taking appropriate steps, and measures at a time to solve. This includes President George Bush after September 11, 2001 creating the U.S. Department of Homeland Security. Even President Barack Obama with U.S. Attorney Eric Holder have not created an observed solution for a certain amount of diversified conditions of anger which has been observed in Ferguson, Missouri, Chicago, Illinois, and other cities and states.

My opinion is that all government officials need help from logical professionals, logical public and private business, and citizens considering how to guide people out of an environment of violent crime. These are issues that have led to conflicting violence in Detroit, Chicago, Gary, and other municipalities. This is conflicting where numerous young black Americans, white Americans, and Hispanic American people have been involved in murders, or are murdered in violent conflicts.

These issues of violent murder, and its level of psychology started hundreds of years ago, and has now (c/o 1990 to 2010) become out of logical control. This has effected all nationalities of people including America's assassination of the 16ᵗʰ, 25ᵗʰ, & 35ᵗʰ Presidents of the United States -- Abraham Lincoln, William McKinley, and John Kennedy. Also this includes the Reverend Martin Luther King considering all of these 4 important men were assassinated by angry people. Since then, America has somewhat struggled to become more socially productive, and moral apart from these conditional acts of anger with violence. Therefore similar to any form of anger, and social conditions of people living together hopefully within the concept of a well-developed society, we can or will maintain and or improve domestic tranquility for the people, and the progress of our American society.

As the 1990s were moving forward a certain amount of destructive acts occurred. This was different from a vast amount of other countries that are not as well developed, but in America numerous acts of violence within anger, and sometimes with the help of technology have taken a toll on the population of numerous cities. Gary, Indiana - Detroit, Michigan - and New Orleans, Louisiana (contrary to hurricane Katrina) are a few cities whom lost large amounts of their population to anger, gangs, and violence which was mostly the result of a high rate of homicides. Chicago, Philadelphia, and Los Angeles are cities with similar concerns, and all these cities have endured domestic murder with occasional suicide. Most of these cities had more casualties observing the consideration that some days of violent fatalities had exceeded the military casualties in the "Iraq-Afghanistan and American" (2000s) engagement of war.

The Oklahoma City bombing was a tremendous issue within observing Timothy McVeigh and even Terry Nichols whom were former U.S. Army veterans who became angry at the United States government. Timothy McVeigh's anger was geared towards the Federal Bureau of Investigation (FBI) whom conducted a raid on the Branch Davidian led by David Koresh in Waco, Texas. Therefore this senseless act of violence was part of personally motivated issues causing metal anger. The motive was to send a sad, revengeful, and hateful massage to an enormous amount of American citizens of how government can control a conflicting level of enforcement through government resources.

The United States government prosecuted four people involved in the Oklahoma Alfred P. Murrah federal building bombing. Besides the death of federal workers this U.S. federal building had a daycare center full of children whom were part of the 168 fatal victims. Timothy McVeigh was punished to death, and then executed federally in the State of Indiana. Terry Nichols received life in jail, and Michael and Lori Fortier received lesser sentences of punishment for not alerting law enforcement. The comparison of laws is and has become extensive, but the violent death of so many American people with the fatal explosive destruction of this federal building became a top priority of extensive concern.

Following the Oklahoma City bombing a certain level of anger, and madness in America occurred. This included the 1999 Columbine High School shooting disaster which was a tremendous tragedy that left 12 students, and 1 teacher dead. The 2 students responsible for these tragic acts of fatal violence with 24 other students injured was committed by Eric Harris, and Dylan Klebold whom during this issue of anger instigated violence, opinionated web site activities, and violent video game reviews.

The format of government after the Columbine massacre became confusing about what should be done to reduce or eradicate this level of anger. Upon this understanding with a sad level of violence that perpetuated a severe condition of unhappiness in a rural community outside of Denver, Colorado and its federal offices, was part of a vital wakeup call. This was vital upon becoming important legislative issues of awareness to com-down this increasing level of anger concerning what states a citizen lives inn, and is video game technology a critical problem. Then this even included a federal law upon which people had to be 18 or 21 years old to purchase violent video games which is to observe or regulate a means of psychology mixed with artificial intelligence. These are a few consolidated issues of how a vast amount of violent crimes are occasionally instigated. Therefore this was a factual issue of concern that anything of disaster could or may occur.

Some of the instigated violence of common concern consist of no motive for Eric Harris and Dylan Kelbold to commit such a massive crime. This has been observed with compounded indifference. Also contrary to the concern that they were young men that had been in trouble with the law before, then other conflicts occasionally seem to keep them quite angry as they committed this extensive act of violence. Understanding this these young men had been angry for a certain amount of time with conflicting issues that they seem to have had trouble in controlling. Then this conditionally became a concern within the use of guns, technology of video games, violence, destructive rap music, sexual violence, and illegal satellite activity.

As the American society tries to help troubled young, and old people turn their life around to live a responsible life, certain technology and even internal medicine have not always been the best or only solution. Contrary to people that had to regroup their constructive thinking within living, or as other people wear fighting as victims that had no intentions on a life of crime, corrections of domestic tranquility were vital. Then numerous conflicts including a communication spectrum became part of a tremendous factor of madness within people transcending themselves in, and out of more so a life of crime, or tremendous disasters becoming a discretionary way of life.

As an indifferent factor, some medical conditions of concern existed with Eric Harris having been prescribed the medications Zoloft, and then Luvox. Contrary to these facts, they had a determination to pursue such things as learning to build bombs, and to consolidate experiments with dangerous, and high capacity weapons. This was observed with the 4 guns that they used to commit this violent criminal act of anger at Columbine High School. These were products of advanced technology contrary to anything like commercial satellites, upon which the many valued issues of technology can occasionally be fatally harmful.

The guns that Harris and Klebold used in the Columbine shooting consisted of an Intratec TEC-DC9, a Hi-Point 995 Carbine, a Savage 67H Pump-action shotgun, and a Stevens 311D double barreled sawed-off shotgun. These are detailed weapons upon which logical regulation is vital. Then observing other conflicts of this crime, the other weapons that were present in this attack also consisted of 99 explosives, and 4 knives. Therefore these weapons and the thought process of these young men were part of them acting somewhat similar to the thought process of Timothy McVeigh, Terry Nichols, and terrorist. This was the observation of April 1999 compared to so much harm 4 years after that tragic day in April of 1995 in their neighboring state of Oklahoma at the Alfred P Murrah federal building.

Over the last 10 years (c/o now 2014) the most critical "mass murders" within violence have occurred in rural towns that have occasional business stability, and business expansion concerns. As these massive issues of violence have occurred, almost anywhere in America has become a potential concern for conflict. Also this is different from places like the Silicon Valley in California where the computer industry is a major resource of opportunities, and valued computer business expansion. Contrary to gang violence or hate crimes throughout the races (c/o black, white, or other nationalities) being sporadic and different from industry, this level of anger in America consist of various problems that are extensive with madness and then violence.

Due to animosity, hate, and anger various matters have exceeded our common welfare, and most concerns of expanding in justifiable decency, and some concerns for business. This includes with a vast amount of tax revenue being generated for city infrastructure projects, school expansion, and improved social standards which hopefully keeps anger, and road rage at low rates as well people working. Causing problems to the common welfare to various people is also becoming a conflicting issue that applies to some of the worse conspiracies in American history. Then as some of the major corrections will consist of various people working together on most issues of prosperity, domestic tranquility, and not domestic destruction to the American society we may can have more workable components of value.

As domestic tranquility is part of important values some issues like a South Carolina Church shooting during June of 2015 has given America additional worries. This was the sein of 9 black Americans being shot to death by a radical young white man named Dylann Roof. Considering his strong racial hate for black America people, it was definitely a hate crime in one of America's safe establishments of worship and prayer.

Observing mass murders and violence in America there are at least 4 things that can cause a diversion of unstable psychology to the people apart from domestic tranquility. These are things of immaturity, and misguided decisions from a diversified group of people. Also sometimes occasionally destructive and indecent information from the internet, and "illegal and hazardous" commercial satellite use that has lately been out of control. Some of these issues are factual violations of numerous executive orders, (c/o Art 106 a U.S. Court Martial offence) that has not been enforced good enough, and can be occasionally inadmissible to destroy foreign enemies, and now American citizens which even includes small business startups or business expansion. Therefore the recent U.S. Presidents of Barack Obama, George Bush, Bill Clinton, and other U.S. Chief Commanding Officers have signed Executive Orders of this critical law, but enforcement has been somewhat nonexistence.

Contrary to gangs, numerous issues of anger and violence which is somewhat and sometimes unexplained with no logical motive for the death of innocent people in America especially with Article 106 violations of law have been out of control. Then as some people have observed various factors about a vast amount of mass murders, this has been considered with the majority of these crimes being committed by a diversified group of people, and the complex logic of a motive which is almost illogical or somewhat nonexistent. Most of these people that have committed or commit these acts of crime are not mostly poor people that are homeless or distressed about money. Understanding this a motive of uncontrolled anger exist within the consideration of how some technology can be a mood altering issue of human destruction.

As a person has been prescribed a psychotropic (mood altering) medication, sometimes Illegal and Hazardous Commercial Satellite use is also more powerful to control, and can severely alter a persons taught process. These mood altering issues being adjusted to certain dangerous levels are unfit or are occasionally unstable for a majority of people in our American society. Contrary to these facts there is medicine that can also kill a person (contrary to illegal drugs), and this conditionally is making prescribed medication also a dangerous issue. Considering this issue of harm Satellites and Lasers becomes just as dangerous, if not more so to maintain a stable environment, and society. Therefore the concept of crime (c/o even medical malpractice, and or a prognosticated illness) some fatal negligence can become an issue that the courts, and the judiciary should have evaluated with logical corrections.

The anger and shooting violence at Columbine High School, the Amish school house shooting, the Virginia Tech shooting, the Sandy Hook shooting, the South Carolina church shooting, and the U.S. Naval Yard shooting were extreme tragedies in the American society that have been complex to understand a logical motive. These tragic events in different states in America have occurred with the misguided observation of diversified psychology, evidence, and sometimes technology to be presented to the courts, and with various details of these crimes. Then the individual state governments argument has not always been clear of all reasons why this continues the happen, therefore we are far from a solution to this crisis.

As local and state government can't find motives for violence, and even if they done something to provoke violence or financial disaster they don't easily admit there wrong doing. The severe nature of these school shootings and other mass murders becomes crimes observed by the U.S. federal government with the increased concern of this frequent level of violence. Then all their resourceful evaluations have not come up with a logical psychological motive, a crime issue motivated be technology, or a corrective answer to eradicate this "Looping crisis".

The consideration that various people have been part of unlawful investigations are occasionally provoking issues of violence, as they factually have only reviewed these peoples history with alternative "indirect" motives. A logical observation leads to the format of an Endless Loop Crisis (c/o unlawful commercial satellite use) which continues to destroy various parts of the American society of innocent people. Otherwise this includes other people that may not have committed such a crime if certain high tech violations of law, various conflicts, and or negligence had not provoked or instigated such madness.

A Northern Illinois University shooting occurred on February 14, 2008 when Steven Kazmierczak a senior at the University who shot 6 people to dead, and left 21 other people injured before he killed himself was another mass murder and issue of conflicting anger. This started at an auditorium lecture facility named Cole Hall with around 120 students in and out of the facility. The violence started during an oceanography class which was in session, and full of students. He entered the class at 3:05 p.m. and positioned himself on a stage with 3 semiautomatic hand guns, a 12 gauge shotgun, and then started shooting into the crowd.

As he wore a T-Shirt with the word "Terrorist" on the front during the Northern Illinois University shooting incident, years before he had some temporary metal illness treatments as he was occasionally unruly at home years before. He like another graduate student: Gang Lu in Iowa who committed the same type of violent act at the University of Iowa in 1991 had given some signs of an Endless Loop Crisis of violence. This observation has been tremendous between these 2 acts, and other issues of violence over a 17 year difference in times of massive anger.

Some of the most destructive ideas included a former Army official Melvin Banks (supposedly CIA), William Daly (corporate & government official), and others like bad judges, law enforcement officials, lawyers, and even unsecured investment bankers. Then as William Daly went from Ameritech to the U.S. Department of Commerce he had no ambition or employee compassion of protecting U.S. Commerce Secretary Ron Brown within his fatal international travel incident. Ron Brown, and a host of other people died in a fatal airplane crash a short time before the September 11, 2001 terrorist attacks which was added negligence or basically an unsolved crime.

Understanding the shooting level of violence at places like Virginia Tech the diversified issue of nationality hopefully should not have led to such a severe conclusion. Upon this observation a factual concern like the 9-11 Report of terrorist attacks left out various corporate and government officials that helped victimized citizens, and people on U.S. soil. Then as certain important national security issues went unconsidered, 10s of thousands of American people were killed and suffered. Occasionally these were satellite oriented crimes committed by angry, or deceitful people that provoke others including terrorist to commit non-motive acts of crime, and or violence.

The people with satellite access that provoke others to live rational are sometimes full of Unconstitutional hate, which even occasionally includes destructive animosity. This understanding including certain citizens (being part of victimized intimidation) seem to cause innocent people to have NO or Very few Constitutional Rights. This is observed "while" Spy's and Terrorist make some Americans commit the worse crimes possible with the manipulation from American people like M. Banks and W. Daly whom committed counter-intelligent violations of U.S. law. These are crimes, and conflicts which causes an extreme level of harmful problems to American concerns. Then as inadmissible conflicts are instigated these levels of observed admissible destruction have become a tremendous level of unlawful instigated manipulation. Therefore this is a problem within a lack of U.S. Constitutional Liability Rights and the Sovereignty of most American people.

Between the Middle East, Korea, Mexico, and various other countries whom also had access to various Federal Communication Commission (FCC) regulated equipment, a tremendous amount of mental, physical, financial, and fatal harm has occurred. These are issues contrary to the last 5 U.S. Presidents of Ronald Reagan, George Bush (1st), Bill Clinton, George Bush Jr., Barack Obama and their FCC Chairman's. As the appointed FCC officials have a duty to outline regulated wired and wireless communication systems, various Communication Spectrum issues, and satellites occasionally has become a major task, and duty of occasional misguided means of competence. During this time some of the FCC Commissioners of concern have been people like Mark Fowler (c/o the Fairness Doctrine), Alfred Sikes, James Quello, Reed Hundt, William Kennard, Michael Powell, and the present Chairman Thomas Wheeler.

Along with incomplete FCC regulated enforcement a communication spectrum has partly caused the American society to witness the most tragic massacres in U.S. history. This is similar to the Virginia Tech massacre with Seung-Hui-Cho harming so many ambitious college students in America on one campus. Understanding these concerns contrary to the FCC, the FBI, and other state and federal government agencies these lawful or logical enforcement resources of America has a Constitutional duty to maintain domestic tranquility. Therefore this shooting and massacre by Seung-Hui-Cho whom was a senior at Virginia Tech located in Blackburg, Virginia was far from American domestic tranquility. Upon this observation he had finally or conditionally committed a massive "terrorist type" of crime that Americans must be alert, astute, and sadly observant about.

Seung-Hui-Cho, an international student, and citizen recently from South Korea killed 32 people including himself (c/o kamikaze war fighting) contrary to a considered mental illness on April 16, 2007. Observing this act of anger and violence during April 2007 (which is a sad reminder of 2 other incidents during the annual months of April) was tremendous on the campus of "Virginia Polytechnic Institute and State University". This international and U.S. domestic issue became one of the worse violent acts committed on a college campus in American history by one individual. Then as he killed himself the motive for this violent act became clearly unknown to Americans, and "Slightly" the U.S. government.

Considering the Virginia Tech issue and massacre was not an aggressive effort by government to enforce existing laws concerning satellite use, or more so terrorism; "tremendous problems" occurred. This was vital, when various laws had an understanding to be disastrous "especially" if they are not enforced. These are laws to be observed and enforced with logical awareness by most all officials of the United States government, but a variation of people between Arizona, Illinois, Indiana, Michigan, New York, and some other states have endured conflicting, and destructive ideas. Therefore even observing conflicts in numerous states, massive shootings have occurred at a capacity of being murder suicide issues within unconscious motives.

Understanding the actions that Seung-Hui-Cho had taken on this tragic day during 2007 on the college campus of Virginia Tech was unfit to the American society. This can be observed as an issue that foreign or domestic terrorism or Illegal and Hazardous Commercial Satellite use can provoke someone to destroy the U.S. Constitution's domestic tranquility. Observing this the Sandy Hook Elementary School shooting massacre committed by Adam Lanza also provided an awareness that America is having a problem with the true existence of domestic tranquility. This act of violence occurred in Sandy Hook, Connecticut on December 14, 2012 which was shocking to Americans due to young children being shot to death.

Observing the Sandy Hook Elementary School shooting with certain research about psychology and illegal and hazardous commercial satellite use the killer Adam Lanza was troubled from a young (adolescent) child. Considering the tragic day of this violent act, 20 year old Adam Lanza killed 28 people (c/o mostly children) including himself, and his mother

Nancy Lanza. This is the observation that the American society was part of an Endless Loop Crisis during the 20 years of his life. Therefore this was a serious concern that I recognized within William Daly of Illinois (c/o Ameritech), Melvin Banks (c/o Army), and others whom were causing as much harm as possible with the use of illegal and hazardous commercial satellites.

An equation between gang violence, and the violence at Sandy Hook Elementary School are issues of similar domestic tranquility conflicts. Adam Lanza was diagnosed with Asperge syndrome, schizophrenia and other mental health medical concerns. Unlike some gang members (c/o young people forced into crime) Adam Lanaz had no "criminal record" prior to this act of violence. Considering this factor, another issue was that the Lanaz family lived near the "municipalities" of Sandy Hook in nearby Newtown, Connecticut with a population of 28,000 people whom had only 1 homicide over the 10 years before this tragedy.

Contrary to homicide and murder/suicide these statistical facts have led me to strongly believe that illegal commercial satellite activity caused some violent acts, and more so various issues of infant mortality. These issues of infant mortality occurred throughout numerous regions of America. This occasionally can be almost as dangerous as the deadly compounds of enclosed carbon dioxide. Some of these infant babies that died I believed were exposed to Illegal and Hazardous Commercial Satellites. Then contrary to the child, or any adult supervision which becomes an occasional attribute to their mental, and physical health if they survive, becomes a vital issue to correct.

The evaluation of mental and even some physical health being a tremendous concern is an increasing problem from illegal and hazardous commercial satellite use. This illegal use of commercial satellites has occurred with "some other children with disillusions" similar to Adam Lanza whom did not improve mentally, and did not occasionally survive with other victims. Then during the year 2007 an enormous amount of infant mortality occurred in Gary, Indiana and other American cities. These 10 to 15 babies that died in Gary was tremendous with only "one" that I can recall that was shot to death, and one in a car accident with illegal drugs and alcohol involved.

Also observing the year of 2007 being a tremendous problem with commercial satellite use, the economy, and the amount of infant babies that died consisted of none or very few publicly outlined causes of economic failures or infant death. These two factors within crisis concerns are similar to the problems of the 1930s Great Depression, but only with severe negligence and conflict. Then even if parents are slightly negligent similar to financial problems, and did not take the highest precautions for their children, the risk within problems increased. Therefore these issues that are rarely discussed in the American society, and then government duties become a critical problem, the crisis gets worse if these problems are not properly addressed.

During October of 2006 an Amish community in Pennsylvania (Lancaster County) consisted of a gunman named Charles C. Roberts IV retaining a school house class room full of children hostages. Then he shot 10 girls between the ages of 6 thru 13. As five of these young girls died from the West Nickel Mines School shooting, he then turned the gun on himself, and committed suicide. Considering this was a community with religious and secluded values, a vast amount of people observed this strange changing condition of events concerning this man Charles Roberts, similar to others that harmed innocent children and people. Observing how various peoples moods were changing similar to how some commercial satellite activities can effect everyplace, and every minute of a day, a person may encounter more issues than any human can handle or endure at one time.

Another violent and tragic act of fatal anger was the United States Naval Yard shooting near Rhode Island in Washington D.C. during September of 2013. The shooter was Aaron Alexis whom clamed to hear voices occasionally before killing 12 people at a Washington D.C. ship yard where he worked for "Hewlett Packard" as a government contractor. Also Aaron Alexis like millions of other Americans was considered a good guy with an increasing interest for guns. The guns he used on that day in September of 2013 was his own Remington 870 Express Tactical (sawed off) 12 gauge shot gun, and then he took (Richard Ridgell's) a fatally shot officers 9mm hand gun, and continued shooting until he was killed by police. Apart from his use of guns, and the type of weapons Aaron Alexis had, he was part of a group of Americans that committed a massive violent crime with no logical motive.

Aaron Alexis was observed occasionally by his heart broken and confused mother as a dangerous individual upon which after his death, she said he now won't harm anyone else. This was part of her tremendous grief for the victims. As his violent rampage of killing was factual, it also was apparent that he had been maybe "locked or trapped" inside of a "Communication Spectrum" and possibly forced to commit a violent act like others whom killed a massive amount of people. Understanding this like him being locked into an illegal voice generated spectrum chamber similar to a gas chamber, a person is trapped without scientific legal, or regulatory support. Therefore him and others have no easy way to solve their problems (c/o hearing voices) in a way that is consistent with logical scientific-principals, or the Domestic Tranquility that the U.S. Constitution grants all American citizens.

This issue of a "gas chambers effect", or a "communication spectrum chambers effect" is part of an arbitrary problem that may have effected more Americans than we closely can understand. The concept of the Communication Spectrum to be trapped inn is a highly inadmissible observation to the courts without good expert witness testimonies. This issue has been conflicting until someone's life (mentally or financially) is partly or totally destroyed, and which is still very complex to prove in a court of law with no affirmation (apart from court room interrogation) from others as complex issues.

These issues to prove in a court of law also will no doubt, and upon reasonable doubt will have a few diversified ways of prosecution consist of lawfully affirmed testimonies. A vast amount of judges similar to Karen F. Wilson of Gary, Indiana has often told people that they must wave their state and federal Constitutional rights is a troubled and conflicting decisions which some people had to make. As this occurs various Constitutional rights are being violated that makes those people, and their families vulnerable. Then (contrary to their 5th Amendment rights) them being vulnerable to any level of "involuntary servitude" the problem gets worse even as she or other government or corporate officials are occasional suspects without true business competitive disciplines.

Contrary to being trapped into involuntary servitude, and being victimized or trapped into a wireless communication spectrum (c/o the FCC) the U.S. Department of Defense, and numerous Americans have suffered with serious attacks, and extensive violence. This has been vitally important since 1990, and maybe before or when the Federal Communication Commission had allowed or did not enforce confidentiality, and commercial airspace regulation. These have been sad problems which are vital to our American Constitutions domestic tranquility, and prosperity. As the U.S. President is the Chief Commanding Officer of the United States Department of Defense, the Separation of Powers have not held up this regulatory issue in various regions to the best levels of duty, and potential for the American society of assets, and more so the people.

The two recent shootings at the Fort Hood military installation in Texas is a major issue, but this is only part of other tragic concerns throughout the United States. These 2 tragedies at Fort Hood consisted of numerous shooting victims which occurred in November of 2009, and April of 2014. Then this has been a mixed consolidation of different issues with similar deadly results including mostly military personal, and some civilians injured or killed.

The first recent disastrous attack at Fort Hood on November 5th of 2009 was closely and conditionally argued as an issue of work place violence, and more so a terrorist attack. This act was committed by Nidal Hasan a U.S. Army major and psychiatrist. Nidal Hasan shot and killed 13 people upon leaving 30 others injured. His motive was considered an act of Jihad upon which he had involvement and "Email" correspondence with Yemen-based Anwar al-Awlaki whom was "observed, and monitored" by various National Security Agency (NSA) officials. Considering this observation within the actions of a U.S. Army psychiatrist a condition of insecurity has been displayed about for the American society of Psychiatry and medical professionals. Therefore this has been part of supporting an enemy foreign agenda which has caused numerous problems for American born citizens even as they were business owners.

Understanding the resource of professional standards in the American society this is part of a valuable concern within a level of appropriate conduct, and a resource of overwhelming occupational knowledge. This truly becomes the logic of issues that even Americans that are licensed engineers, lawyers, accountants, doctors, and others like sociologist or even U.S. Intelligence officials as government have not did enough to stabilize acts like what Nidal Hasan did on the military base at Fort Hood. If the American society including all resources of state and federal government officials can not keep a military base safe, we definitely have a problem keeping the rest of the American society within assets, and people safe.

This conditionally has been the concept of various people in America supporting an enemy foreign agenda. Then this has been observed as international investments, with international terrorism. Even as we are reminded of the September 11, 2001 terrorist attacks, and even terrorist hijacking airlines during the 1970s, and the 1980s the American society of people, and more so government has excepted levels of complacency. This is complacency that takes Americans backwards by government not being alert, or insuring domestic tranquility or other constitutional values about these issues. Also these are and have been harmful problems even as the American society has numerous levels of technology, social standards, and government to prevent such acts of harm to any logical factor of the American society becoming disastrous.

Another "Endless Loop Crisis" issue and level of violence occurred at the Fort Hood military installation on April 2, 2014. This was a violent shooting that specialist Ivan Lopez committed within killing 3 people on this military base, and injuring 16 other people. Also this isolated and conflicting act of tremendous harm and violence on an active, and resourceful U.S. military base was the observation of a crisis that the American society has to correct. Therefore even "post traumatic stress syndrome" dose not seem to cause a "person or solder" to commit this type of radical act within violence.

As the concept of mass murders in America has increased over the last 25 years to disastrous proportion within people like Ivan Lopez whom have committed crimes without clear motives, this is clearly a crisis, and an apparent concern. This crisis has continued over and over without lawful or logical solutions about why so many people posse this level of anger. Even as America has lately made an effort to prevent terrorist attacks -- the issues of Nidal Hasan, and Ivan Lopez killing their own military comrades has been mixed, but with similar factors of emotional unrest. Therefore if technology is causing mental, physical, financial, or fatal harm; America is observing the results almost worse than any time in American history.

Observing other massive issues of anger in America, some violent acts have been instigated by people with technology, and some were not; but these bloody attacks have become extremely out of control. In 1991 George Hennard killed 24 people including him committing suicide, and with 20 other people injured at a Killeen, Texas Luby's cafeteria. Then years later two people were part of a killing spree with 17 deaths, and 10 people injured. Most of the shooting was by Lee Malvo (17 years old), and planned by John Allen Muhammad a former member of both the National Guard, and faithfully guided by the Nation of Islam. Therefore as two angry individuals roamed through Virginia, and Washington D.C. shooting random victims with a high powered rifle, their act of violence was sadly labeled as the Beltway Sniper attacks.

There were 2 other mass shootings that occurred in 2011 and 2012 which outlined a level of anger in America. During January 8, 2011 U.S. Congresswoman Gabrielle Gifford was critically wounded in an assassination attempt by Jared Loughner upon which 6 other people were killed, and 13 others injured.

Contrary to the Congresswoman being shot in the head, she still survived with enormous medical concerns. Now she is still making progress in her recovery as she is supported resourcefully by her astronaut husband Commander Mark Kelly. There also was a young child (9 year old) Chirstina Taylor Green shot to death, and a federal judge (John Roll) killed in this act of violence which means that some of these victims had very little to do to provoke this level of anger.

A little more than a year later on July 20, 2012 James E. Holmes used multiple guns in a mass shooting in an Aurora, Colorado multiplex theater. His shooting rampage killed 12 people, and injured at least 70 other people in a variety of ways. The massive shooting was a tremendous conflict as James Holmes even dressed up as a Batman villain character, and entered an Emergency Exit before he started shooting, and killing innocent people at a movie theater.

On this day in July 2012 James Holmes entered the stage in front of the crowd of people watching "The Dark Knight Rises" a Warner Bros production, he then started shooting to kill. This production consisted of an updated Bateman film, but the shooters interest seem to be deranged as his hair was died red similar to the "Joker Character" which seem to put his interest in being "Enemy Number One". He was immediately arrested, and has now been sentenced to more than 3,200 years in prison as he was prosecuted for numerous murder charges, and the logic of various mental evaluated conditions. Therefore as an American society with technology, we hope not to advance any additional mental conflicts leading to anger, tragedy, and disasters such as this, and other similar acts of fatal violence to a society of hopeful tranquility.

# TECHNOLOGY IN AMERICA

(3)

# CHAPTER THREE

(3)

Anger and Technology In America

Worse Than The Watergate Crisis, Without Domestic Tranquility

# TECHNOLOGY IN AMERICA

(3)

Observing technology in America which is conditionally a broad subject, an enormous amount of products are sometimes available for use by the general public, or only for people that are lawfully authorized personnel. The concept of authorized personnel (c/o people) usually means the American local, state, and federal system of diversified government employees. These people are to be lawful licensed, affirmative personal that use complex technology properly. Then in a business and industry concern this also consist of licensed professionals, various disciplines of occupations, or occasional citizens of concern which includes students conducting lawful research in universities, colleges, and or professional establishments with business involvement.

Understanding research and other activities surrounding technology the results usually should be safe, and not cause harmful problems which includes instigating anger, health problems, financial problems or fatalities. This becomes the logic of technology in America that crosses many bounders. These bounders within government, diverse professions, or occupations with products, and services that can have diversified good, bad, positive or negative effects. Therefore as bad technology may affect thousands, or even millions of people if not worse with tragedies it can cause Americans to sadly suffer, which lately includes a lack of lawful affirmations, and bad scientific principal laws that apply to vital corrections.

The majority of technological products in America includes the valid responsibility that any activity within use is conducted to be safe for all people throughout America's general public. This issue applies to anything that is consistent with the Constitution of the United States, the Constitution of individual states, and all government matters of logical interest. Then as regulated resources of a broad range of technology can be observed, it becomes important that enforcement "if necessary" is pursued, or any authorized use of technology is conducted with responsible and lawful disciplines. These responsible disciplines are applicable to most social standards and even the complex issue of a communication spectrum with scientific-principals that are, and should be appropriately consistent to the U.S. Constitution.

Understanding the U.S. Constitution with chartered guidance from the U.S. Congress and others a commissioned study (c/o 1999) was conducted as: the "Commission to Assess United States National Security Space Management and Organization. This U.S. Commission to Assess U.S. National Security with Space Management and Organization changes has been part of the effort to improve technological business matters, and "National Security". Then also this includes international, and U.S. domestic businesses or organizations that use "land base or orbital satellites" for communication affairs (a cloud of massive satellite & computer memory), or hopefully activities regulated by the American system of government.

The commission study managed by Linda Haller (Space Commission Staff member), and Melvin Sakazaki (c/o the System Planning Corporation) was determined to observe four important commercial space sectors. These four commercial space and satellite sectors consist of defense, intelligence, commercial, and civil managing issues to govern, and keep organized. These management organizing issues recognized vulnerability, risk, threats, and opportunities.

Understanding these satellite common concerns within daily use is part of "remote sensing satellite services", "locations, navigation including timing satellite services", and "then weather satellite services". Therefore these issues are considered with authority, and are carefully appropriated at capacity level for the concern of "no" unlawful negative potential or any understandable repercussions. Otherwise some repercussions have been undetermined along with the good, and bad discrepancy of artificial intelligence apart from normal human decision making, and active living.

Within the use of various technological small and large communication system products, "national security", and storm warnings are vital. This is contrary to the fact that even more so U.S. domestic use of communication equipment between American corporations and citizens becomes a positive factor, but also can instigate or cause anger, and other diversified problems similar to "aggravated disruptions". Considering this necessity (c/o government regulated concerns) the use within products that are unlawfully active can cause the appropriated lawful use to be "flawed and somewhat destructive".

The concept of effective electronic technology use with inflationary prices goes back to the first car phones, VCR's, even the Volkswagen Beatle automobile caching on fire, and thousands of other good, and or bad products going back many decades. These industry objectives were part of products that took years for certain technology items to be widely excepted in the American society. Even the telephone, electrical power, and satellites have become part of this type of technology revision, upgrades, and market values with various industry, and government standards including Constitutional laws which apply. This understanding can be relevant as part of lawful product and service concerns within society, and not to be a destructive resource of unlawful activity.

The amount of technology that is established every year in America can conditionally be the equation of advanced production within industries, corporations, and most colleges or universities that study technology for improvements. These are well considered establishments that do research to help develop various technological items, and systems for safe transportation, communication, weapons, and other industry and government valued duties with systems of mass proportion. This then is even factual within corporations like General Electric Corporation, Raytheon Corporation, General Dynamics, and others whom mostly have been productive U.S. Department of Defense, NASA, NOAA, or the National Weather Service contractors.

Some of the most advanced levels of technology during the 1990s, and the 1st two decades of 2000 have been used by various professions, some citizens in unprofessional ways, and or within unlawful activities. Understanding this, various issues including Americans spying, plotting to steal or commit fraud, and or committing defamation towards other Americans has become a tremendous problem at record rates with additional mental conflicts. This is part of an Endless Loop Crisis with no lawful "Affirmation" except but to cause complex damage.

Occasionally an Endless Loop crisis consisting of Illegal and Hazardous Commercial Satellite use has caused a negative impact to 10s of thousands of American people or more. This destructive impact within violations of law have instigated violence within people being murdered, or part of financial crimes, and or fatal industry issues of negligence. Then if satellites are used properly this becomes part of an advanced society with properly shared information, communication, and other electrical values within technology resources of discipline.

Contrary to most occupations, and professions finding use of the latest well developed technology, certain industries have taken negative advantage of the American people. These are industry concerns like banking, telecommunication, broadcasting, computer science, internal medicine, accounting, engineering, and others that have found good, and bad issues of technology use. Some of these issues of use have went from a controlling subject of business, money, sex, religion, and other personal or private household issues. Therefore this becomes vitally important where the 1st, 4th, and other Amendments of the U.S. Constitution has, and can be "abused".

The occurrence by various people, professionals, and or even certain American enemies (foreign and or domestic) have engaged in conflicting issues of a negative technology collaboration. Contrary to U.S. Department of Defense issues there are occasional products developed for massive technology interest, and sometimes to secure the "Common Defense or General Welfare" of the American people, and society. Understanding this from U.S. President's George Washington to Barack Obama and the future observing the Common Defense, and Promoting the General Welfare was considered positive, but occasionally complex which today has slightly become negative with bad technology use. Then observing mental, physical, financial, and fatal harm from satellite users the U.S. Constitution would then become a positive document of livable progress.

Contrary to this fact William Daly with Ameritech Corporation, Karen F Wilson (a Judge / Mayor), and others between Indiana, Illinois, Arizona, Michigan, and even New York have used Illegal and Hazardous Commercial Satellites against U.S. Presidential Executive Orders. Then in America and other well developed countries the logical, and lawful use of various means of technology can be positively helpful, and not harmful if regulation and enforcement is astute with disciplines for the people.

International and more so U.S. domestic crimes with slight levels of legislative satisfaction in technology considering satellites used by Google Earth, or various television and radio networks with meteorology equipment is a severe conflict "if used wrong". Observing this concern, the American system of government has not seem to prosecute any spy's except in New Mexico's, Los Alamos National Laboratory, and various foreign terrorist included in the 9-11 Report attacks. This facility in New Mexico out of a vast amount of other U.S. government facilities consisted of vital experimental technology, and some national defense computers coming up stolen, and or missing which has caused serious concerns. Therefore people of a U.S. domestic and international capacity may have been part of using stolen equipment that is hazardous to numerous other Americans as this is indifferent with the occasional complacent opinions of some parts of the U.S. government.

Understanding complacency, various factors of some technology within, and by the use of conflicting people which includes government, did not save lives, or prevent the death of thousands of American people. Also this includes the destruction or damage to some businesses during 1990 to years after 2001. These fatalities even with the inclusion of disaster by terrorist organizations on American soil was a problem. This complacent issue was clearly observed within the September 11, 2001 terrorist attacks, during Hurricane Katrina, and a vast amount of other severely tragic fatal manufacturing, and industry explosions or accidents apart from government conflicts.

Considering certain facts about technology protecting American citizens we occasionally observe anger or complacency from small and large businesses including an extensive resource of government. Most times this becomes a destructive condition which eliminated various disciplines and a logical format of U.S. Constitutional domestic tranquility. Then as some of these issues of technology like within commercial satellite use, an enormous amount of the time it seems that this technology has destroyed citizens or caused severe asset damage. Therefore if any form of technology is going to be more helpful and productive -- it must be used properly, and lawfully. Other than that these can be destructive conditions to Americas domestic tranquility, and even the prosperity of the United States which has pushed numerous cities throughout the American society full speed backwards.

Some of the most publicly used technology has been guns, cell phones, laptop computers, tablets, and faster computer servers which supports the good, and bad of the internet. Then various connections to orbital, and land based commercial satellites including drowns has been part of National Security with conflicting issues of good, bad, or unlawful technology that is sometimes not enforced effectively. Apart from the issues of Edward Snowden whom released millions of peoples personal and government emails, this seemed less harmful then at least hundreds of other Americans instigating unlawful and illegal conflicts. Therefore these are vital concerns that apply to confidentiality within the Constitutional rights of American citizens.

The vital difference of Edward Snowden was that the U.S. government did not say or outline that he caused metal, physical, financial, and fatal harm to numerous people. His conflict has been observed with unlawful technology use causing a serious, and personal information crisis. Then as some government and corporate computer systems store so much information about millions of Americans this becomes an issue of conflicting access. These issues of access within good, and conditionally bad Americans and or international people sometimes becomes part of a destructive concern of defamation or manipulation causing misunderstood disputes.

Observing technology in an international capacity (c/o American research with advancements in medical and satellite technology) these become two broad subjects. Also within the more than 100 members of the United Nations the concept of good, and bad satellite technology, and internal medicine has extreme levels of concern as it applies to diversified industry standards along with national social standards. The American medical industry has established way more pharmaceutical products to hopefully implement medical solutions especially as this is compared to some commercial satellite industry products contrary to an overall network of services. This is factual as various countries other than, and somewhat including the United States can achieve enormous medical, and satellite technology advancements. Then this becomes vital without harm to the American people, and with compliance to the U.S. Constitution.

Numerous advancements like "Military Drones" consist of various resources, and industry values of technology ranging from communication satellites, satellite imagery, weapons using satellites targeting systems, to transportation satellite systems" which may be combined. These concerns become part of a tremendous amount of technology subjects "besides and including time of war conflicts" with communication, imagery, and transportation supporting American troops. Therefore with drone technology this becomes an issue of location, navigation, and timing satellite services which is vital to safe air, water, and other U.S. transportation or even communication values of direction.

A massive amount of issues within communication satellites and other technology issues has been considered lately between the United States, England, Germany, and a few other countries. This becomes a format of good, and sometimes bad technology that has effected massive amounts of people. These people are rich, well off, and even the indigent of poor people competing against major nations, between certain corporations, and government with extensive resources of technology. Then understanding this concept of air space, and technology management within the organizing of regulated activity by the American system of government, this becomes not just a tremendous problem, but a vital necessity to lawfully be corrected "even with" legislature.

Another possible corrective matter and major issue which includes argumentative technology concerns have been the Medical Expert VS the Engineering and Commercial Satellite Expert. American doctors of internal medicine continue to create new diagnoses for severely ill patients like with Parkinson disease, and other neurological or even mental health disorders where a cure most times has not been determined. In true values a cure is very complex, but this has been a normal conflict for decades. Also in the courts more medical experts are used for legal cases such as mass murders, or domestic murder with or without suicide. If the defendant in these cases hears voices or some other procurer condition, satellite experts have not been considered if this technology (c/o hearing voices) has helped instigate a certain level of violence.

Communication, telecommunication, and even the internet are occasionally complex industries to argue in a court of law, and or to control all appropriate regulation. The Federal Communication Commission (FCC) has only regulated major communication industry businesses with "less extreme" enforcement. This is a factor with more satellite activity and some electronic uncommon devices such as those remote flight controls that operate public, private or government drowns which would be in conjunction with the U.S. Department of Transportation.

Another FCC societal, and technology issue includes vulgar and negative subjects within public television viewing or radio listening content that was not allowed for years, and decades ago. During the 1990s up through 2000 the American system of government allowed this to be unlawfully destructive with legislative issues like the Open Sky's policy (c/o air travel) which was slightly different to Rupert Murdoch's (c/o Europe) Sky A & Sky B communication network projects for satellite access.

This also included bad rap artist, people that wanted to sexually dictate woman, or be involved in violence, and even commit financial fraud as government officials or investment banking institutions. Otherwise what seems to be an Open Sky issue to slightly control various regions of America far outside of the boundaries of the U.S. Constitution, and other laws in various states has become a crisis. Then as satellite technology and social media has been used to promote or instigate conflicts or even violence the FCC missed, and ignored certain vital matters. This was vitally observed at local, and state agencies which has a vital duty to enforce decency, and some confidentiality law resources.

The concept and understanding of the Communications Act of 1934 which was amended by the Telecommunications Act of 1996 was to appropriate reasonable rate charges. This was regulating a logical service to all people as telephone customers which became important, except for what could be a disaster for certain other citizens. One factor of those disasters applies to the United States Codes (47 U.S.C. subsection 151 and Article 106 of the U.S. CMM) as a Court Martial offense with legal importance to the United States, and it's Constitution. Then this vitally included Presidential Executive Orders that were violated.

As these issues of Presidential Executive Orders apply to unlawful technology (c/o satellites) these violations become an issue that is out of an uncontrolled capacity with no prosecution or hardly any governed affirmation similar to no hazardous or danger warnings or even a legal court ordered warrant. Then numerous violations of these laws have become part of destructive conflicts, and the courts occasionally ignore their duty to review all legal concerns or arguments with effective disciplines. Therefore this becomes factual upon how most lawyers don't work on these various cases, considering (business or government) with any helpful expertise on these subjects. Then as lawyers and other professionals not working hard at these cases; or if ever to argue this type of case in the lower courts, to the higher courts of law, ordinary people will questionably live better. Therefore they will be less likely to be victimized, and maybe not end up being destructive or complex defendants in crimes similar to some recent mass murders or other diversified problems.

The most destructive and violent conflicts observed within anger, technology, and how people hearing voices suffer seems to include or be partly an issue caused by certain technology government oversight diversions or conflicting liability. This part of an increase in the dissatisfaction of social values, and conflicting technology includes complex product liability issues that have caused massive and misunderstood tragedies. These technology issues also include "the more satellites added into the commercial airspace, the more problems of un-affirmed voices seem to be heard unlawfully (c/o causing mental harm) in the airspace, along with other problems. Then Americans must observe that these un- affirmed voices being heard by numerous people are not from "Martians", Poor people, people who are Deceased, people in outer-space, or even people from another Planet. These are the voices of people with livable resources of money, and or are people whom might be instigating a conflict to the person's hearing those voices.

As these voices are not the communication issues of people in Heaven or Hell, but those of unlawful or hazardous communication satellite use, these are activities by various destructive people whom need to be prosecuted similar to the Watergate Hearings. Considering this fact, numerous small communication companies were in and out of business causing more harm than any logical good. This is conditionally how some neighbors spy on each other at the highest point, and violate laws of confidentiality with total silence in our airspace which has suffered from some Open Sky A to Z issues. Some of these businesses started from former associates of large companies like Comcast, AT&T (c/o Ameritech), Verizon Communications, NASA, NOAA, the U.S. Department of Defense, and others with certain business, and technology values including access to government agencies. Most of these corporate businesses along with government do have similar capabilities of technology which provides knowledgeable experience. Then their inappropriate activities of consolidated experience can be a hazard to normal life, and living along with other people that instigated tremendous conflicts, and problems.

This issue within problems of lawful enforcement even against Corporate America, government officials, and or various individuals has been ignored which has caused numerous American people to suffer mentally, physically, financially, and even fatally. Also this became part of expanded problems of insecurity, vulnerability, and extensive negligence. These were activities mostly with small apparatus communication, and satellite systems used by numerous people. Therefore they have then found ways to instigate massive social problems in America worse than other times in history, observing "destructive time after destructive time".

Very few communication companies like Ameritech with the destructive activities of William Daly of Illinois, and a few others have not been prosecuted for complex crimes that him and others committed. This is also observed while he along with other Indiana government officials (c/o David Capp, Kim Robinson, Karen F Wilson and a few others) have used satellite technology to destroy citizens lives. Then this destruction also includes various families other than their own. Considering these complex violations of law they also should have solved any problems within who was the worse violator, even if they were supporting foreign enemies which provided evident years later in 2001.

These became family issues of destruction which consisted of them using Illegal and Hazardous Commercial Satellites to cause distractions to "peoples professional, and social ambitions" in Chicago, Northwest Indiana, and other American regions. Understanding this these conflicts within problems sometimes included manufacturing explosions, and the destruction of marriage between a man and woman. Observing the issues of technology and marriage between men and woman their ambition to have a good attitude that includes a loving relationship became part of severe distractions, emotional harm, and even more the destructive exploitation of woman.

Observing technology that destroys the ambition of any man, woman, and or child has been occasionally an inadmissible conflict (c/o admissible outcomes) with not many people truly having an opinion of understanding. With this logic a vast amount of understanding mentally without any clear determination, motive, or evaluation is part of an expanding crisis. Then this becomes observantly vital to a person making a "good or more so a bad" decision, and therefore with this -- the American system of government has failed numerous citizens.

A critical problem is observed when government in America does not know if they want to get something done "lawfully or legislatively" to solve a crisis concern of a massive amount of angry people. Other than that more young, and some old people will be loss, or sadly die because of these lack of governed regulatory duties. Then as this issue of unlawful commercial satellite use has caused tremendous conflict within a vast amount of people barely understanding the effects of this technology, it consisted of destructive levels of conspiracy to control people unnaturally.

As some technology conditionally observing guns, and more so communication satellites or other satellite systems have been used unlawfully, this has destroyed a normal way of living in America. These are facts upon when, and how some people have used the most powerful weapons to shot the youngest, and most innocent of children in America. This includes numerous people due to gang violence, and mental behavior which them, and others sometimes observe or consider as unnatural with confusion. The concept of any advanced technology in America or worldwide is usually created to consist of logical, and or more so "natural control". Then this is where conflicting resources of harm can't be prevented due to issues that cause "step by step" severe damage or problems.

Conditionally two industry issues that the United States is still very good at is space travel, and predicting dangerous weather. This is due to the National Weather Service along with the National Aeronautics and Space Administration (NASA), and the National Oceanic and Atmospheric Administration (NOAA) as this research is direct with "scientific U.S. government duties". These regulated duties have kept America astute, and alert about various subjects of danger. Contrary to danger the issue of bad, or destructive people with access to certain technology (c/o satellites) at this capacity is a tremendous conflict that only causes massive confusion. Then the people have suffered at record rates of distraction, and or destruction that became imminent to normal life in America.

Between the two activities of NASA, and NOAA (c/o the National Weather Service) deadly hurricanes have been predicted 2, 3, or more days in advance. This was observed with hurricane's Katrina, Ike, and tropical storm Sandy along with other complex disasters like tornados. The most complex "Emergency Warnings" in America is still tornados (c/o twisters) due to the fact that they develop quickly, and can cause severe damage with fatalities similar earthquakes. These are dangerous issues which are part of "weather satellite servers" that provide a warning to direct citizens. Considering these facts, technology should be used for lawfully logical issues, and the most dangerous, and hazards issues within emergencies along with a secured infrastructure.

As the most complex issues of hazardous weather or even issues such as predicting terrorist attacks have been vital concerns of the U.S. government, some other conflicts have not been observed with efficient disciplines or lawful care. Then issues like corporate or citizen concerns with some government values have failed to prevent financial disasters. This becomes the concern that some of Americas technology has not been used to its best lawful ability, and professionals sometimes must play a role in a way that is not destructive. Therefore this vitally includes how competitors in business have government rule and regulatory responsibilities to abide by.

Within various concerns numerous American cities have only went full speed backwards with bad political, and government decisions. Observing this good, and more so bad technology issues of destructive use of various products have become conflicts which have been a critical concern to domestic tranquility, and has had an economic effect on America's prosperity of sovereignty.

The use of bad technology against normal American living standards, contrary to the bad of foreign dictators like Muammar Gaddafi, Saddam Hussein, Idi Amin, and others in undeveloped countries whom have caused great harm is a diversion of numerous other people with destructive ideas. Then this becomes especially true if we compare foreign and U.S. domestic relations (c/o United Nation matters) with issues of even big business, and government. Therefore understanding anger and technology in America we have social values to go forward in a positive and rightful way, and not the wrong way even with the good, and massive issue of technology or conflicting immigration that Americans have endured with various dangerous conflicts.

# MOTHERS AND FATHERS WHOM KILLED THEIR CHILDREN

# CHAPTER FOUR
## (4)

Anger and Technology In America

Worse Than The Watergate Crisis, Without Domestic Tranquility

# MOTHERS AND FATHERS WHOM KILLED THEIR CHILDREN

(4)

A sad crisis within the American society has occurred over the last 20 years that is a tremendous problem to most marriage or household values throughout the United States, and a vast amount of families. This issue is the lost or diversion of Domestic Tranquility to Domestic Murder which on rare occasions consist of suicide. Then this becomes an Endless Loop Crisis of psychology by not ruling out discretionary anger, but with bad technology government oversights. These are oversight technology problems like computer and satellite crimes, and destructive negligence which more problems can arise. Even bad usage of communication devises with foreign or U.S. domestic radio and or television, certain conflicts can be provoked, or instigated to cause domestic disaster.

Observing the valid crisis of woman and men that kill their children, and or families numerous instigated conflicts must be reviewed, if possible. Then contrary to the many issues of anger some households or families throughout America have suffered worse than various times in the history of the United States. This becomes indifferent from the many fatal shootings in cities like Chicago, Illinois, Gary, Indiana and others that have consisted of the killing of numerous innocent children and other people. Therefore this crisis is at the extent that certain families almost no longer "exist", or they are part of a severe format of people trying to regroup.

The tremendous rate of domestic murder in America has become an increasing problem to the extent that some woman have killed their children with conflicting, and an unconscious understanding within logical motives. These violent crimes have shocked communities at record rates similar to Andrea Yates of Texas whom drowned all 5 of her young children in 2001. Andrea Yates unlike some others that committed such violent acts did not seem to clam, to be hearing voices, but she did seem to clam, that Satan influenced her children to be bad. Therefore her, and her husband Russell Yates went through a tremendous amount of changes as he tried to

47

help her overcome mental conflicts, but the outcome continued to become disastrous.

Andrea Yates was punished to life in prison (c/o parole in 40 years), but the sentence was overturned due to an inaccurate expert witnesses testimony. Then as she was released with the agreement to be committed to a Texas mental health treatment facility she is still being evaluated for various concerns due to the unlawful actions that she committed. This was due to a Plea of Insanity with an observation of more corrections in her and some others crimes of similarity. Apart from any corrections of these acts of violence and anger will require very extensive, or special incarceration even with the logic of an appeal. This is due to the fact that it becomes difficult and complex for these people to return to society, and face opinionated people who remember their acts of anger and or madness.

Contrary to numerous psychiatric medical evaluations these resources of violence are part of someone whom may not have understood anything of an unlawful discrepancy within bad satellite or communication technology causing severe harm. These technology flaws or violations of law can provoke harm or instigate problems that take up extensive time (c/o managing any income) as certain social or household conflicts are most times made worse. As this applies to Andrea Yates this could have been a long term problem within how Illegal and Hazardous Commercial Satellites can cause a mental illness. Then as this Endless Loop of technology can be used for years without government enforcement, and or corrections various problems sometimes get worse overtime.

As Illegal and Hazardous Commercial Satellite use is not conditionally a clear fact of everyday evidence with Andrea Yates, and some others it certainly is a real possibility observing the crime or acts of violence that her, and others committed. Observing years later in 2005, 2006, 2007, and 2008 a rational amount of domestic murders in Northwest Indiana and other states seem to be part of an Endless Loop Crisis where I recognized commercial satellite activity was completely out of control. Besides an enormous amount of infant mortality throughout Indiana between 2006, and 2007 two woman, and a few men committed extensive acts of domestic murder with one person that included suicide. Contrary to a vast amount of suicides like in Evansville, Indiana where during 2007 some 40 deaths consisted of suicide, and this problem became a severe crisis; there has been no newly directed legislature or very few if any court hearings, that have provided helpful solutions.

Throughout Indiana one shocking case after another has occurred. The issue of one violent act of anger consisted of domestic murder when a mother killed her children which was observed within Magdalena Lopez of Dyer, Indiana. She killed her 2 sons that were the ages of 9 and 2 years old. She reportedly used a baseball bat to beat them to death. As she was sentenced to 110 years in prison, the concept of pleading guilty with a mental illness became an extensive argument with plans for an appeal. Between her and her husband tremendous conflicts occurred, but the most traumatic is that she also mentioned the Devil or Satan as a conflicting motive. Therefore Haven, and Hell are not that close; compared to an Endless Loop of unlawful satellite or even computer use. This effects a vast amount of American citizens as this problem seems to consist of additional emergency needs of government enforcement within the "Constitutional boundaries of technology".

Another mother that killed her four young children (by strangulation) in Elkhart, Indiana was Angelica Alvarez on November 14, of 2006. As the facts seem to include that Angelica (27 years old) killed Jennifer Lopez (8), Gonzalo Lopez (6), Daniel Valdez (4), and Jessica Valdez (2) as the prosecution became aggressive and or accretive. This could be conflicting upon which the prosecutor Curtis Hill took up a normal logic of madness before prosecuting the case that was somewhat relevant and appropriate. Contrary to the Elkhart, Indiana prosecutor Curtis Hill seeking the death penalty, U.S. Immigration officials had inquired about the matter with the Mexican consulate. Understanding this the U.S. and Indiana Constitution has been severely violated with needs of an enormous court dispute that could be appropriate to some solutions for this crisis.

Understanding the defendant Angelica Alvarez, and the prosecution led by Curtis Hill an issue of why is this level of domestic murder becoming so extensive has only somewhat been considered as a slight crisis. This was observed, considered, and written about with certain local newspapers, occasional other media outlets, and not enough corrections of logical enforcement from government during 2007 up to these present years of 2016 and the future. Therefore contrary to any satellites, conflicting technology, or psychology that may have been a factor -- the good, and bad opinions within the abuse of woman, some men, and especially foreign specking woman has been somewhat observed.

Observing a father that became severely disconnected to normal life in Griffith, Indiana consisted of Mickey Gordon killing his stepdaughter Jessica Janusas whom was a, well liked high school cheerleader, and softball player. This occurred on June 11, 2007 with her being shot to death, and him (her stepfather) being found dead with a single bullet shot to the head. A factual law court observation is that besides a younger son in the house that was not harmed when this type of murder suicide occurred there is very little left that the prosecutor or lawyers may have to argue in any form of government. This is relevant unless they can determine or investigate a solution to what led to this factual level of anger, and violence.

During August 7, 2007 Kevin Isom of the Miller section of Gary, Indiana fatally shot his 2 stepchildren, and his wife Cassandra Isom. Considering this triple domestic murder one child's age was 16 years old Michael Moore, and the other was 13 year old Ci'Andria Cole as this tragic act of anger with domestic murder was part of an ongoing threatening crisis. Kevin Isom supposedly made a statement that: I Can't Believe I Killed My Family" when being arrested by police. Considering Kevin Isom did not kill himself, when he was arrested his statement to police would seem like an "Unconscious" statement for someone that had occasional "Clear Vision".

As a few other domestic murders occurred around the same time (c/o East Gary) with a woman and child being murdered as they were beaten with a bat by the father whom has on occasional times - as the defendant complained of hearing voices. Contrary to this fact during the trial of Kevin Isom the courts did not seem to conditionally mention or evaluate him for hearing voices. The conditional problem of people hearing voices becomes a factor of; "mental conflict" or "a mental disturbance" which leads to instigated mental distractions within decision making such as when "Total Silence" is a direct order in school. Therefore as "Total Silence" and "Total Confidentiality with logical Affirmations" are outlined in schools and other places as the commercial airspace is different within the U.S. Constitution (c/o Indiana's Constitution") this violation can destroy all Constitutional Domestic Tranquility.

A mix (c/o Constitutional Disciplines) of being conscious, and unconscious with conflicting thoughts (c/o Technology) is almost like "Sleep Walking". Contrary to this Kevin Isom killed everyone in his Miller apartment, but he did not kill himself. This seems to be a level of indifference that the courts have a chance to determine what went on with his decision making during this outburst of violence. Contrary to a vast amount of crimes or even negligence, this issue of anger with tremendous violence was far from what most Americans try to live by within "domestic tranquility". Then apart from the good, and bad of achieving prosperity -- more people, professionals, and government officials must work together on the best possible solutions and corrections.

Considering these facts, the case consisting of the State of Indiana VS Kevin Isom went on for 5 years with a vast amount of mental health evaluations, and rulings of a mistrial. These court proceedings seem to not give a better determination of him being provoked to this level of anger except economic losses, and or maybe his own animosity. This is part of the issue within dispute between Kevin Isom and Cassandra Isom whom was 40 years old which is 1 year younger than Kevin Isom at 41 upon which he was rational about being unemployed. Cassandra Isom was a church secretary and she was paying all the bills, but as he was a former security guard with a vast amount of guns becomes part of the consideration that he did not seem to commit the violent crime of armed robbery for money. Therefore as he committed a vicious crime of murder, the only conflicting resolutions that have, arise within why he could not come to any better decision is a strong scientific mystery.

The issue of technology has numerous conflicts within the madness that society can provoke, but how it can be prevented is even more complex. This becomes almost as bad as the sale of sex, romance, and derogatory or explicit music on the radio over the internet and or other forms of communication. Then this becomes the good, and bad conflicts of law disciplined values through the internet, and other communication systems. As issues of madness in America have occurred which seems to be part of numerous conflicts including anything of anger and certain conditions of technology the changing times in America has a lot of government business to conduct. This becomes a vital understanding for massive amounts of people to survive without violence.

A valued level of psychology (with occasional technology) is observed to understand why is this anger or violence so rapid over the last 25 years (c/o 1990) in disastrous proportion. This consideration of concern is part of the level of manipulation, invasion of privacy, and even issues of conspiracy to instigate explicit conflicts of interest. These are crimes pursued from certain technology which has been used as part of a severe, and complex rate of violations of law before some people with their not-so-complex equipment are prosecuted. Therefore this crisis has been tremendous with conflicts that can cause depression, and even more so anger.

The concept and definition of "Depression" is complex apart from the definition of "Anger". As it applies to a person's emotions 2 out of 4 interesting definitions of Depression consist of the act of pressing down;

lowering or shrinking; which is also considered "a low place". Also depression has a meaning of; low sprits which is part of sadness or gloominess that goes along the statement that failure usually brings on a feeling of depression.

As it applies to "Anger" this definition consist of the felling that one has towards something or someone that hurts, opposes, offends, or annoys another; or a strong displeasure. Also being "Obsolete" with Angered grief; is trouble which goes along with the logic to make angry; arouse anger in "certain subjects or someone". Then understanding these two definitions the issue of conflicts or illegal and hazardous commercial satellite use that causes a person to hear disturbing voices can instigate these emotions extensively

The format of emotional disruption and or annoyed irritation of depression on occasions is sometimes that a vast amount of people can not easily overcome this uncomfortable emotion, unless anger is a relief. Then this level of anger is produced in a destructive order apart from vital means of protection. To overcome depression a person has to determine a solution to eliminate whatever is causing the resources of that present level of depression. Then the person has to figure out; is it something that they can do by themselves or is it vital to get help from someone else that is helpful or positive that won't instigate or provoke anger or worse such as acts of violent crime. This becomes factual in this day in time as the logic of how every American should be concerned about Constitutional Domestic Tranquility and their prosperity.

Observing depression, anger, and domestic tranquility the concept of technology in America has to hold the highest values of lawful liability without too much artificial intelligence. Satellites and computers are based on electronic and electrical (c/o communication) activity which also goes along the determined factor that these levels of technology can cause a "lack of full sovereignty". Then a lack of full sovereignty eliminates prosperity and opportunities to gain or manage any level of wealth, as this causes the American society of people to go backwards. Therefore in a court of law one of the main objectives with satellites and most times computers is that "courtroom" inadmissible evidence must be argued, and proven to be admissible. This even includes without reasonable doubt for the lawful progress of a well developed society.

To understand the last 2 decades of the 1990s and 2000 certain issues of satellites and even computers have consisted of crimes worse than the Watergate Crisis of 1972. Contrary to the Watergate crisis consisting of at least 7 men using "Electronic Surveillance Equipment" unlawfully; today (c/o the 1990s and 2000s) more unlawful use of satellites, and computers has destructively occurred. This has created thousands of households, and or small businesses suffering from "Watergate Type" of violations of law. Then today as anger and technology becomes part of a crisis similar to Watergate, this crisis and problem is now effecting thousands (1000s) of citizens at a time. Considering this concern the courts have larger duties then Watergate along with most legislature issues that have not been workable.

An Indiana University Law Professor Marshall Seidman outlined in a book: The "Law of Evidence" that Judicial Notice can appropriate "indisputable evidence" in a trial court. Also the formatted matters of Judicial Notice by trial judges take observed notice of "scientific-principals, historical facts, geographical facts, and political facts". If appropriate hard work is a commitment by a lawyer of professionals like engineers, "then" these issues can become indisputable evidence. Observing this without some of these legal disciplines by the courts, responsible lawyers, and other professions (c/o some Doctors, Engineers, and Computer Programmers) the concept of technology may continue to instigate the worse crimes possible. Therefore this is a problem locally apart from how things occur in Washington D.C., and various parts of the U.S. federal government.

Observing the courts with the logic of Judicial Notice as it applies to today's laws becomes violations that are "Worse than the Watergate Crisis". These two (2) legal and "judicial notice" factors of importance are the conditions of scientific-principals, and geographical facts. The scientific-principals, and geographical facts are vital with the present capacity of advanced technology in America, and how it effects people in all regions. Then various regions consist of the appropriate concerns of how the laws, and certain professions are valued or respected to the safest levels of domestic tranquility.

Political facts and historical facts are important judicial notice concerns that apply to the past few years with more violent acts of crime than ever in the history of the United States. This problem is vital which includes most regions of the United States being effected. Then the political facts consist of who is responsible, or workable as it applies to overall government duties to correct problems of regulating, and or prosecuting these conflicting matters. Observing this, these are issues that are part of any argument in the courts (c/o some politics) like in Watergate with a special prosecutor named Archibald Cox whom became vital.

Now with this level of an Endless Loop crisis (c/o commercial satellites) throughout the United States this will possibly need more special prosecutors as it becomes a vital requirement within solutions. This requirement with their duties including expert witnesses in a geographical, and scientific capacity are vital to help the people that do not understand whether the crisis is mental health or "irresponsible" satellite communications. Similar to the Andrea Yates case, the Aaron Alexis case study, and the Kevin Isom case if - the only expert witnesses are doctors: the courts are leaving out 4/5ths of other important professional experts out of the equation. This is valued within issues that are good, and bad, or these issues are ruled at severe levels of additional crime or negligence. Then this makes it important to solve certain legal disputes, and social problems that most times turn into a crisis part of a Constitutional Law solution.

Understanding mothers or fathers that have committed domestic murder with occasional suicide, and their children or others that are dead, it's appropriate to say that they suffered from a lack of full sovereignty. Even in a few cases a son or daughter has committed these violent acts of domestic murder from the consideration of mental health by a few other people. As a level of sovereignty is recognized between the 1990s, and the 1st and 2nd decades of 2000 a lack of full sovereignty has been observed with madness due to financial and social matters. These are issues that have taken the United States, and its citizens full speed backwards as far as World War II (c/o the Great Depression), the Vietnam War "and even of the Revolutionary War".

Upon the observation that any person close to being an adult can commit violence, and even domestic murder with occasional suicide has been an increasing conflict and problem. This has been factual as the American society has been going backwards which consisted of some of the worse acts of violence than any time in American history. Conditionally murder is not a crime that has just began to occur, but the enormous rate and amount of violence lately has caused a tremendous loss to the population in a vast amount of American cities. Between Chicago, Detroit, New Orleans, Philadelphia, and Gary, Indiana they have loss at least 50 percent of their schools. This is due to the lack of enrolment within students which outlines that the rate of violent crimes is part of this critical equation which has caused a tremendous reduction of families, churches, schools, and most normal ways of living life.

Observing the American people for the last 20 years, and the U.S. Constitution over the last 2 centuries has been part of a vast amount of issues which seem to be making America worse than a 3rd world country. This has seem to be an issue with inter cities that are falling apart with abandon commercial and residential facilities including severe losses to these regions population. Therefore as violence and anger increases a vast amount of cities consist of communities that are not cared for by the people, and dangerous infrastructures becoming worse with a lack of funding, and organized discipline.

The lowest rate of domestic murder has been observed by a vast amount of new citizens to the United States. This includes people from the Middle East, Mexico, Korea, and others similar to terrorist groups. These are people that don't kill their families, but go out and kill innocent Americans. The 9-11 Report of terrorist attacks, the Virginia Tech shooting (c/o Seung-Hui-Cho), the Boston Marathon bombing, and a few others are important examples. Then as they did not kill their families, it seems that the highest rate of mothers or fathers that are killing their families are frustrated as born in America citizens.

Understanding anger and violence by people of a U.S. domestic, and or international capacity is causing the American society we live inn - to go full speed backwards. The international hereditary conflict is that some people say that this is how they do things in the country they are from. This is similar to some of the worse undeveloped countries on the earth. Otherwise lawful government corrections are vital before America is in a complete stage of self-destruction.

# MARRIAGE, RELATIONSHIPS, AND VIOLENCE

## CHAPTER FIVE
### (5)

Anger and Technology In America

Worse Than The Watergate Crisis, Without Domestic Tranquility

# MARRIAGE, RELATIONSHIPS, AND VIOLENCE

(5)

The concept of occasional or long-term romantic relationships, and or marriage which sometimes includes a circumference of good, bad, and or conflicting values has recently become a crisis concern. This has effected a vast amount of people in more so an "unnatural American lively hood". As an Endless Loop Crisis is complex to control, major problems have been part of men and woman becoming stable couples. Otherwise as this has been observant in numerous American cities and towns with low rates of men and woman getting married with happiness, the diversion of vales have endured tremendous conflict.

Lately (c/o the 1990s and 2000s) technology has sometimes played a critical role within problems of personal values in America. These conditions which includes technology use - besides positive or productive resource concerns have been issues that create additional anger, destructive conflicts, and sometimes even violence apart from normal (men, woman or husband and wife) relationship differences. Most of the time this becomes a technology conflict which is unlawful to people, and can instigate or provoke serious problems when most Constitutional laws are being severely violated. Observing this tremendous enemies (c/o black, white, or other Americans) becomes a major effect to what's considered "domestic tranquility and or holy matrimony".

Contrary to men and woman engaging in loving relationships, the issue and rate of marriage throughout the United States from 1990 to 2015 has lately been at conditional, and historically low rates. This seems to be a bad problem due to men and woman that can't come together to form marriage vales of a commitment for life to each other. Therefore occasional anger or strong disagreements become severe even with too many outside opinions, which occasionally includes some harm to any children that may be present. Then as a dead man or dead woman are not capable of marriage numerous murders has eliminated a massive amount of people. Occasionally this sometimes has been the result of Illegal and Hazardous Commercial Satellite use which cause people to hear conflicting or destructive (airspace) voices causing disagreements. Then this has led to the antagonizing aggressive nature of people willing to commit to violence for their own pleasure and destructive ways, therefore making society unstable.

Observing the issue of mental and physical anger or violence between man, woman, and certain young people over the last 2 decades (beginning slightly before 1995) has been severely complex with diversified repercussions that sometimes leads to death. As more woman are having children outside of wedlock their logic of marriage vaguely seems clear to occur. This even includes how some woman more so have attempted or even have killed their children, spouses, or lovers. Then this is due to some woman more so whom have a level of frustration which becomes a serious problem, and crisis apart from them most times not being committed to a secure marriage. With so much anger in America a vast amount of men have also committed similar crimes, or conflicting acts of violence as this becomes a crisis that needs a logical government solution.

Understanding these concerns Illegal and Hazardous Commercial Satellite use (c/o technology and scientific principals) can create issues that are tremendously worse without logical or productive thinking. This has also been the creation and instigation of angry people that was comparable to a level of hate and animosity within people like William Daly of Chicago to cause other American people suffer, and American born business owners to "suffer". Then a judge/mayor of Gary, Indiana Karen F Wilson, and others have supported an enemy foreign agenda against these same established Americans. Therefore by supporting a majority of Middle Eastern gas station owners this has caused destructive or complex control within some American values. Otherwise we must remember that now we as Americans are at war against people from the middle east and our level of caution must be astute.

A certain amount of conflicts and crimes consist of a few factors that have led to extreme problems like the terrorist attacks on September 11, 2001. These were terrorist attacks that a vast amount of citizens, and more so government officials said or instigated that we don't have to worry about until it happened. Considering this an enormous amount of children loss their parents in these attacks. After these tragic attacks including various relationships and marriage conflicts the American society and government have only slightly recognized some of these vital issues. Then with bad technology certain levels of political, government, and business decision making has fallen to all time low levels that is destructive to the American society of people, and the prosperity of the country.

Contrary to an expansion of homosexual marriages, the concept of men and woman having a sound sense of love, and conditional financial or economic resources, enormous traditional values have suffered. These traditional values like home ownership being a commitment to overall family disciplines have decreased as people using commercial satellites illegally have increased in the American airspace. Therefore good, bad, and conflicting technological use consist of a vast amount of repercussions. Observing this, the repercussion is an objective of rich or poor economic factors of living or managing livable, and normal standards.

Another repercussion which has become a tremendous problem in the American society is part of ethical and professional standards. This becomes the logical concern that only knowledgeable, ethical professionals, and people know what may need to be done to lawfully correct technological problems and the social conditions of a crisis. Observing the United States Constitution is also a strong concern that effects these resources of ambition that is established for financially rich, poor, and all people or citizens. Then these diversified people must make decisions to live in a law bidding civil society. Considering this, these are values that are vital to be workable, and conditional as it applies to men and woman having logical resources of prosperity, and or good relationships which requires a level of common sense.

As the economy in America has been a severe issue of conflict for a vast amount of normal citizens, and a substantial amount of businesses this also has made relationships and marriage a complex commitment. An enormous amount of the time this includes defamation, and occasional negative opinions from other people. This becomes the fact that more married couples do better when there is love, concern, economic values, and financial security in the relationship, and or marriage. Contrary to this fact some levels of depression like with Andrea Yates, and the ambition of her former husband Russell Yates consisted of them both having an education to earn a good living but that did not give them holy matrimony. Otherwise the concept of economic stability is conditionally ruled out in this concern of a legal case as he was a NASA Engineer, and she was a registered nurse.

Within the concept of marriage and relationships some conditional values of the Constitution's 1st and 4th Amendments which applies to a combination of "religion, speech, privacy, and affirmations" has somewhat destroyed various issues of "holy matrimony". This destruction has occurred with some of the lowest rates of church marriages in American history.

For men and woman to achieve holy matrimony a relationship must be respectful and appropriately responsible within shared commitments. Therefore other people with unlawful technology, and some economic conflicts of concern can keep couples from living in normal ways of good decision making which is an extreme loss of determination at its worse.

Considering a vast amount of mass murders were committed by people out of wedlock a severe distraction has occurred contrary to people like Andrea and Russell Yates and others that suffered domestic violence, and or murder. As Russell Yates was a NASA Engineer these considerations of what Illegal and Hazardous Commercial Satellite use can do destructively is not just a mystery, but a scientific concern of technology principals and 4th Amendment domestic household values. Observing scientific principals and any concerns that can be destructive, a vital issue consist of a collaboration of professionals (c/o government committees) that must be established. This must be done appropriately with logical ways to explain, and outline to all levels of citizens, and government the nature of this problem and scientific crisis.

An observation within the Yates tragedy occurred when Michael Powell was the Chairman of the Federal Communication Commission. This was a concern which consisted of the changing times within Americas communication infrastructure within overall telecommunication and communication technology. These changes become tremendous with numerous values of telecommunication technology in the various ways people communicate and have responsible agreements or an understanding. Considering this, these changes were more so with cell phones, the internet, and broadband which satellites and a communication spectrum are the least understood, and can be both intricate (c/o complexity), and intrigue (c/o secrets or unlawful activities). This issue of concern within all parts of society considering the outcome of a vast amount of social standards with diversified results has become a crisis worse than the Watergate scandal which includes or requires government corrections. Then these become corrections for most all parts of the United States including all American values of government, and the people.

The Federal Communication Commission (FCC) has and becomes one commission that is largely nationwide or one of the last organizations of government that is expected to help both intricate, and intrigue relationships or marriages. Contrary to these issues that become values of confidentiality, even with bad rap music, and destructive issues concerning the internet a vast amount of conflicting issues apply. Between the FCC, and other governed operations like the International Telecommunication Satellite Organization (INTELSAT) in America, and its collaboration with other countries, they are starting to be concerned about various OPEN SKYS policies. Then these policies and technology become more intricate due to complex arrangements, and intrigue issues due to secrecy or unclear crimes. Therefore these policies can affect any, and all citizens throughout most airspace regions of the world, and discretely the United States in good, and bad ways.

In America, and more so England; the News of The World issue (c/o Rupert Murdoch) with the Open Sky's policy has become vital concerns along with "Sky A and Sky B" projects. These satellite projects consist of airspace satellite systems that the News Group Newspapers with Rupert Murdoch promoted years ago. Some of this activity was part of a "Phone Hacking" scandal against a British teenager named Milly Dowler who was later found dead. Then this has included other people throughout England, and America occasionally trying to have relationships, and or a marriage which (c/o commercial satellites) most times end up with violence or bad arguments. These are arguments that men and woman have which should be part of understanding each other. Also this is part of their commitment within love and or a relationship capacity of values, contrary to the lawful uses of satellites like within proving news stories, sometimes instigating harm, and or conditionally predicting weather.

Observing the case of Kevin Isom and Cassandra Isom of Gary, Indiana their relationship and marriage ended in the worse, case and scenario. This has been the case with hundreds of other issues of domestic murder, and or with occasional suicide. As these tragic results of a marriage or relationship ending with violence the Constitution of Indiana, and the United States rarely argued to correct this extensive problem, and crisis. Considering this, domestic violence continues to destroy people, and families at massive rates which means holy matrimony will almost become non-existent if this crisis is not corrected.

If technology and scientific principals had been part of various acts of domestic violence the courts have not used professionals outside of Law and Internal Medicine to understand or apply a logical solution. The format of corrective solutions applies to other professionals may consist of engineers, scientist, and manufactures of satellites to have government standards of human improbable safety.

As it applies to various resources of technology the lawful use of various diversified activity in society, and the overall commercial airspace is tremendously important to evaluate and observe. Telecommunication, communication, and wireless technology systems have expanded into this level of access within millions of good, and bad people in America, and worldwide. Therefore in some sense it's not complicated to understand the concern that people will use these levels of technology to harm other people, and or even dictate men, woman, and or even relationships in an Illegal and Unconstitutional capacity.

Observing the courts, and the U.S. Constitution holds powers of responsibilities, the equation of separated powers are valued within executive, and more so the legislative branches of government. This becomes even more important when it comes to legal discussions of technology with the courts "whom some would say satellites are a crazy idea and logic of legal discipline with American technology. In logical comparison the 9-11 Commission was established due to a terrorist attack by foreign enemies that did not harm their own families. Contrary to this, even Americans like Adam Lanza whom killed 28 people (c/o mostly children) at Sandy Hook Elementary school, he started with killing his mother.

Considering terrorist did not kill their families Adam Lanza being one of a few who committed mass murders that killed a parent is a complex sign of severe anger in America. Understanding these issues the American society can only work hard to understand the logic of changing or correcting this problem. This sometimes goes along the anger of most gang violence as some people have tried hard occasionally not to have so much destruction in their everyday lives. Therefore various conditions of anger are taking parts of America in a bad direction of sometimes no return.

Manipulative people with technology and sometimes the use of guns altogether can cause tragic problems that can not be solved easily. This may include threats and intimidation causing people, and families to be vulnerable. A legal conflict "That I Observed" was " Manipulation, Invasion of Privacy, and Conspiracy" which is complex (similar to the Watergate Crisis) to prove, and or even sometimes tuff to fight through. Therefore this is the observation of sometimes massive amounts of people locally, and a diversified level of people throughout the American society having been victimized. These are complex victims as citizens with occasional technology which has effected them, or has caused them or numerous people to suffer.

Another legal concern is how America maintains domestic tranquility that is helpful to men and woman relationships, and marriage. Domestic tranquility dose not consist of violence, and constant anger. This becomes the fact of a bad attitude or technology that can increase anger. These are issues which needs to be corrected through governed legislature at a state, and the federal capacity which may include the courts. As domestic tranquility is threatened America is losing a logical way of people to peacefully work together with respectful ambitions. Then this becomes a concern of how real progress will be established, and maintained.

Considering most issues of marriage, relationships, and violence in the American society surrounding the 2000 millennium has conflicts within the changing times that must be corrected. As anger and technology in America is considered far from domestic tranquility today the format of moral values throughout the United States will have to be reviewed in mind with the effects of technology. This is vital upon how the United States Constitution's 1st Amendment and the 4th Amendment is managed or governed to give the people an understanding of logical respect. Otherwise then, this will hopefully give us productive and workable solitude to this mental, physical, financial, and fatally harmful crisis.

# AMERICAN NATIONAL SECURITY & COMMERCIAL AIRSPACE

(6)

# CHAPTER SIX

(6)

Anger and Technology In America

Worse Than The Watergate Crisis, Without Domestic Tranquility

# AMERICAN NATIONAL SECURITY & COMMERCIAL AIRSPACE

(6)

Observing "American National Security and Commercial Airspace" as it applies to anger, and technology throughout the United States is lately becoming a domestic and occasional international crisis. These National Security Administration crisis concerns of various critical issues has been disastrous, and complex to understand. As an amounting array of American historical tragedies have occurred (c/o the last 20 years) with sometimes massive fatalities, and or economic destruction the American society has suffered in numerous complex ways. These are tragedies that resulted in death, or financial disaster which have caused tremendous grief and anger for various victims, survivors, and families that were effected.

As national security, commercial airspace, and the infrastructure has not been governed with the highest levels of regulated awareness, everyday people have found themselves in a state of confusion. This diversified conflict has caused many people social, economic, and financial hardships. Therefore as some National Security Administration court hearings, and conflicting legislative procedures have been conducted for the concern of a conditional amount of people in America, various social standards have suffered. This consolidation of American people have been destroyed by death, and or financial destruction.

The history of national security (c/o the National Security Administration) goes back to the beginning of World War I in 1917, when the United States government declared war against Germany. During those decades following 1917 to the present time in America, numerous wars and defense missions (c/o WW II, the Korean War, the Vietnam War, the Iraq, and Afghanistan wars) consisted of communication systems, aircrafts, and a vast amount of other products throughout the world. These products have advanced for war, and occasional civilian use especially as it applies to computers, lasers, and satellites that can be helpful, but also destroy normal American citizens.

Approaching the Vietnam War, and the Watergate scandal, the combination of national security with the commercial airspace had become an international, and U.S. domestic issue of regulated concern. One important issue is that the Watergate scandal type of crime has become even more common without a good resource of government enforcement, and or prosecution unlike former President Richard Nixon and 7 conspirators. Therefore some issues from 1920 to the first decades of 2000 on occasion have consisted of good, bad, and out of control technology. Observing legislature this level of activity was different, but similar to the use of the "Atom bomb" which destroys people, and the environment.

In some logical opinions the most critical attacks are through the airspace which can be by the use of nuclear, and or guided missal's being shot at any American cities or other regions of the world. This level of air warfare conditionally may include hijacked airplanes over the recent decades becoming a major threat which the American society has taken more losses then stable existence. The concept of the United States Department of Defense (DOD), and the Central Intelligence Agency (CIA) has technology to help manage, and regulate these issues. Then as they can observe people, business assets, and information throughout America including certain worldwide concerns these become critical matters to keep lawfully in U.S. domestic order.

Contrary to United Nation resources, if these governed technology issues are used wrong, this can be similar to bad law enforcement officials who engage in destructive police brutality. This is vital even as people in America observe a communication spectrum that we are reminded to ask or be concerned if all laws are being respected, enforced, and or honored? The outline of these levels of technology has a discipline to be maintained, managed, and governed with lawfully valued and effective use which applies to any technology effects.

Apart from nuclear weapons or guided missal's an important fact now consist of satellites and radar systems which have become complex to understand their active, and lawful use. Satellites in the United States for decades have been used to track, and intercept enemy missal's throughout the commercial, and residential airspace of America. As certain corporations like Raytheon Corporation with the U.S. Department of Defense have made this a worldwide wartime discipline, conflicting domestic issues have taken away important U.S. national security responsibilities. Contrary to this fact the natural format of humanity within people, plants, and other habitat including the environment are still vital without this extensive technology deception, or inappropriate security values.

These commercial airspace activities conducted worldwide is part of observing most technology resources of the U.S. DOD, and the CIA on regular duties which were then established for America's security within defense. Then this has become a larger part of the North American Air Defense Command (NORAD) which has a duty to detect, intercept, and destroy enemy airplanes or rockets. This becomes the understanding that any enemy conflicts must be maintained, or controlled with logical enforcement, certain upgraded wartime resources, and or lawful disciplines to regain or maintain a normal way of life in America. Understanding the difference of NORAD, a few other governed operations and normal levels of tranquility becomes a factor that should not consist of self-destruction activities, or a conditional level of illogical prosperity.

As NORAD, DOD, and CIA technological systems with some civilians and military officials whom have used them recently, important American national security has fallen to some of its lowest, and weakest levels of security in decades. Contrary to the Pearl Harbor attacks on December 7, 1941 and now the "9-11 Report" attacks which has been a pivotal comparison, America's airspace security is lacking some resources of protective disciplines. These were disciplines of domestic tranquility, prosperity, and other U.S. and individual state Constitutional values which were violated, and totally ignored. Therefore when it comes to this level of civilian, and government concern the courts have a vital duty along with the immediate attention of legislators to make corrections within the laws. This then becomes the concern of an executive order to the control of a mayor, governor, and or a president under the Separation of Powers.

Observing executive orders of a president, the last 30 years with Ronald Reagan, George Bush, Bill Clinton, George Bush Jr., and Barack Obama have been observed with good, and bad conflicts. As they have been part of the Separation of Powers within executive, legislative, and judicial resources, the American society must keep it's people attainable to lawful progress, and advancements. Contrary to the 1940s, 1950s, and up to the 1980s America has been part of certain advancements, and critical corrections. These corrective losses within industry, social values, education, and government standards are, and become part of major changes to cover losses.

Understanding this, America has a diversion on how to use national security executive orders against foreign nations, as some activity of harm in other countries has been conducted against their own citizens. This becomes a vital concern similar to bullies as it applies to instigating bad domestic conflicts of interest. These issues of bad technology use -- was a conflict with President Ronald Reagan, and the former CIA director George Bush which got worse with other presidents over the years of 1990 to 2000.

As it got worse this has been clearly factual within the presidential executive order of George Bush, and Bill Clinton underestimating a certain amount of international affairs which become crucial. This consisted of good and more so bad immigration, and destructive terrorism during the tenure of Defense Secretary Donald Rumfield, and National Security Advisor Condoleezza Rice. These complex national security times consistently sent some American businesses and people backwards including 2 extensive wars in the Middle East, and the extensive cost and anger of wartime citizen indifferences.

National security and defense over the last 2 decades (c/o creating anger) have been full of American failures worse than certain times in U.S. history which has led us to war following the 2001 attacks. These issues with advanced technology have been accompanied by disasters of liability like with hurricane Katrina (contrary to being predicted), the Oklahoma City bombing, the 2 fatal BP explosions (2005 & 2010) and a massive amount of other fatal business industry explosions. These are just a few tragedies that could have been prevented, and which caused an assortment of damage, and anger. This capacity of damage caused a vast amount of American values to be pushed full speed backwards. Then the American system of government has vaguely made corrections apart from continuing to not reduce certain sad levels of grief, and anger.

Observing the United States and various issues of national security which include all financial, economic, and social standards has caused overall progress in America to be slow. This is the destructive concern of people like William Daly (Chicago) of the Ameritech Corporation with other bad corporate officials. Him and some of his constituents used the National Security Administration (NSA) technology against various people, and smaller businesses to support what became an enemy foreign business, and social agenda. A vast amount of these businesses were not even their "communication or business competitors", but only small business owners working to have prosperity. Then most business setbacks (c/o new Middle East gas station owners) took away from the progress of Americans which sometimes take extensive time to recover from these law violations, if ever. Therefore some issues of even financial crimes became severe, and conflicting which effected massive amounts of other people.

Another critical business conflict (c/o an Endless Loop) within failure consisted of thousands of angry senior citizens in America that have lost their retirement savings, and or investments. In America the wrong investors were occasionally targeted by NSA, contrary to Middle East investors that pulled hundreds of millions of dollars out of most U.S. stock exchanges days after the September 11, 2001 attacks. These issues, financial crimes, and conflicts with some foreign investors have forced senior citizens to go back to work in order to survive at an old age. This also has been tremendous to the American society of prosperity values which fall below standards in most major cities. Otherwise a massive issue became the 2007 mortgage crisis effecting most all regions in America, and this also effected business ownership along with certain industrial and residential development properties.

Other crisis concerns includes an enormous amount of immigrants which is a critical problem that takes away young American peoples opportunities, and aspirations. Also conditionally this gives these financially effected senior citizens a critical way to evaluate survival contrary to angry or destructive young people, and conflicting business owners. Therefore these become employment opportunities that keep a vast amount of Americans from creating productive startup businesses. These domestic tranquility, and prosperity values are beneficial to the long-term progressive future of the American society.

As prosperity issues occasionally have been part of different levels of advanced technology that has sometimes not been effective, improperly used, or have not been used in productive ways this has added to major problems that have occurred to some peoples ambition. Indirectly these become issues of severe negligence or complex crimes. This consolidated issue is not to say all technology for national security, and the commercial airspace is bad, but some corrections, and or government oversight are well overdue. An appropriate example is that (c/o the 9-11 Report) the U.S. government found Saddam Hussein, and then years later they found and killed terrorist leader Osama bin Laden. As these were workable U.S. defense matters including soldiers and technology with CIA operational disciplines, this national security progress had made critical corrections and decisions with vital, and responsible effective action.

Contrary to war time issues these are Illegal and Hazardous Commercial Satellite use concerns which have been out of control. As most of these issues are violations of executive orders, they have effected small towns, large and small city living standards for "black American woman and men" that are being torn apart from unjustifiable ignorance, and whom were threatened with conflicts. It also is effecting white Americans at "record or conflicting rates". This is only slightly different contrary to how commercial satellites can affect all human beings. Upon this understanding the problem within Illegal and Hazardous Commercial Satellite use can consist of a "lack of full or logical economic expansion and sovereignty". Then this effects American regions of people from working to have prosperity, and or even domestic tranquility.

As the 1st Amendment, and the 4th Amendment are important, some people, businesses, and certain concerns within government have used commercial satellites on almost everything that does not always help national security. These have been issues of obtaining business, and personal information illegally at an Endless Loop capacity. This information mostly consist of defamation of character that destroys responsible free speech, productive progress, and sometimes this is threatening to our religious values of logical freedom within worship. Contrary to these facts America has suffered record amounts of recent, and diversified destruction.

Some other Constitutional issues have been extreme violations of law to exploit woman into prostitution, and pornography. These and other conflicting violations have included financial concerns, and some violations of insider trading on various stock market exchanges which becomes money that goes in all "good and bad" directions. These overall conflicts within American small business ownership, the destruction of continued education in colleges, and the discrepancy within logical marriage has created a crisis. Then this has made life indifferent for hundreds of thousands of Americans to constantly restructure their lives. This is a sad problem within a crisis that some people in the American society, and the American system of government like William Daly and others seem to accept as a vast amount of the United States is going full speed backwards.

Understanding national security with factual issues of a crisis for men and more so woman to follow a logical format of government has been an American conflict of extreme interest. Even homosexuality, derogatory rap music, and forcing woman to become sex slaves has not helped the stability of marriage or families, and the resourceful expansion of business or good government in America. These unlawful operations or conspired issues have destroyed some men and woman for life. Therefore contrary to acts like the 9-11 Report "terrorist attacks", the bombing of the U.S.S.

Cole naval ship (October 2000) and with other tragic acts that were not prevented, this has been part of needed "government oversight". Apart from other severe problems these are U.S. government failures that can not be repeated (c/o national security) anytime soon, "if ever".

Observing American social values in the 1990s, and 2000s it has become easy to understand how the church rate of funerals has conditionally outpaced marriage between men and woman. These issues have been disastrous with a higher condition of death within confused young people having more funerals then older wise people. These are issues of not just destructive internet activity, but also business, and government officials that have nearly somewhat destroyed an American society of Constitutional law disciplines with slightly unregulated technology.

Understanding Constitutional law issues and violations, certain levels of social destruction occur for the American people, and more so young people that are being pushed backwards and misguided. Considering this fact the American society of people need technology which they understand, and not unregulated "communication" technology that gives the people no lawful affirmation. Then contrary to the older people that understand various parts of the commercial airspace, a diversion of people are occasionally being pushed to the point of no productive return. This is due to a discretionary lawful, and Constitutionally resourceful society that is stuck in crisis mode.

As it applies to American young people, and the most prosperous or conditional business startups, any mistakes, crimes, or negligence has been part of a conflict within logical business survival or existence. Also this exist within a crisis similar to the crimes of Kenneth Lay (Enron Corp), Bernard Madoff, and more so Bernard Ebbers of WorldCom. So as Bernard Madoff was a non-executive chairman of the NASDAQ stock exchange, his influence misguided a vast amount of small expanding businesses (c/o billions of dollars) along with some major investments from prosperous and prominent organizations. Then contrary to Bernard Madoff, and his investment scams later during the 2000s (c/o prosecution), Bernard Ebbers and his communication activities at WorldCom (c/o MCI), and Ken Lay (Enron and broadband) was more of an anti-trust law disaster for small American entrepreneurs, and various investors. WorldCom and Enron in various ways controlled certain activity that the National Security Administration of the U.S. government had problems managing within their regulatory duties.

Observing national security, companies like WorldCom, and certain satellite commercial airspace and various communication spectrum activities consisted of bad or unlawful decisions which caused other tremendous harm with no lawful affirmation. This becomes the fact that a vast amount of new business owners already find numerous problems that can keep them from managing a profitable business. Then with WorldCom and even Enron the resource of communication, and electric utility corporate businesses consisted of extensive oversight issues that caused problems in most regions of America. With people using various forms of technology illegally, various business owners became victims with expenses that are an economic, and financial burden. Obtaining information illegally has been a vital factor, and problem like with unnecessary cost within expenses that becomes a subject occasionally from violations within the 4$^{th}$ Amendment. Therefore this becomes difficult to operate or survive in an economic environment of business, or as a normal citizen.

Understanding national security having tremendous concerns there has been reports of military, U.S. Secret Service, and some CIA officials sometimes not being efficient, or being heavily engaged in bad conduct. This includes prostitution, the abusive use of drugs, and alcohol along with other conflicts. Even more so the 2 shootings at Fort Hood (U.S. Department of Defense) in Texas, and the attacks on the Pentagon (9-11) has outlined a U.S. government defense weakness of critical problems. This is how some issues must change the "strength of defense and intelligence protecting" the American society.

The security of Americans consist of a format within a "strength and equation" for the equality of the American people, various Constitutional laws, and how we must recognize dangerous foreign relations. Decisions such as this means "the People" of America are honored by the U.S. governments "Constitutional Laws" (c/o state constitutional laws), but at the same time eradicating terrorist or dangerous criminals. This becomes a valued, and important necessity for domestic tranquility upon properly enforcing these vital laws. These are factors as it applies to various issues, and technology that are important today, and far into the future with more advanced technology.

Contrary to high level concerns of United States government defense and intelligence operations, some of America's most distinguished defense contractors, and corporations have been part of complex technology violations of law. Raytheon Corporation, Microsoft Corporation, WorldCom Corporation, Enron Corporation, BP (c/o England), and

Ameritech Corporation (c/o AT&T) have committed crimes or negligence that occasionally come close to national security violations of law. Western Union, and the Rand Corporation are similar businesses that have endured these encounters with the U.S. government. This becomes the observation that Corporate America, and other worldwide businesses are not complete strangers to the American system of courts, and our overall government of lawful resource's.

Western Union around the 1920s along with the U.S. government were active in gathering information from American, and international telegrams for defense, and security purposes. This was a consolidated agreement between Western Union, and the United States federal government during the Woodrow Wilson presidential administration. Over the decades within time this was the bits and peace's leading up to the establishing of the National Security Administration, and the Central Intelligence Agency following the Pearl Harbor Attacks. Considering these international concerns, lately an Endless Loop of violations within complex law have caused U.S. domestic disasters at record rates.

The concept of record levels of harm and U.S. domestic destruction within a domestic American Endless Loop Crisis seem to consist of mass murders, domestic murders with occasional suicide, and even provoking fatal industry explosions. This part of the National Aeronautics and Space Administration's (NASA) research and development projects is appropriate within discretionarily being affirmed to the American people. Upon this observation that everyday people don't recognize if there is harm to the citizens, they will occasionally only know about these issues as a vital concern, and a complete warning of described problems. Then this became the American social level of domestic destruction when massive people as law professionals, and oil industry executives and others throughout industry made bad decisions. Also a vast amount of the time these people wanted to dictate, and control other Americans illegally against their U.S. Constitutional values, and business rights as citizens.

As destructive National Security becomes an Endless Loop Crisis of violations of law that most times only judges and prosecutors (c/o the judiciary) can logically afford to argue, a government budget is helpful. The equation of this budget is vital relief as some American values and people have suffered and need support. These are issues to financially argue in the courts to keep prosperity of the law binding American citizens into economic, and social order. Then it should be understood that these people whom allowed these destructive conflicts, and even business transactions to occur should be held accountable even if it's between satellite activity on earth or traveling to orbit and back.

This becomes relevant besides the opinion that someone is considered crazy (c/o an Endless Loop Crisis) for valuable ideas -- especially when they work hard to achieve valuable advancements. Then these factors are a destructive format of a well-developed society. Observing this we must be aware that it was even thought to be crazy for man to land a spacecraft on the moon, and walk in space. As these experimental subjects with other technology advancements has been considered, the good, and bad of technology advancements is part of an enormous network of businesses, and organizations that should not have become too complex to regulate.

Observing the United States Department of Defense and (c/o NASA) some military crimes are becoming complex, and deadly. As Americans honor veterans of foreign wars, it becomes vital to understand this equation which has consisted of some deadly violent crimes, financial crimes, and crimes that have taken the American society of people full speed backwards. These are losing issues especially within allowing the "wartime opposition" to gain control over a majority of America's businesses within gas stations, manufacturing, and other business occupational, and professional establishments.

We as Americans must remember that gas is one of the most dangerous and flammable products sold over the counter to anyone. Then to allow closely connected enemy constituents close too terrorist to control these businesses is part of potentially killing Americans, destroying property, and the recent beheading of Americans in the Middle East. This level of violent terror has effected international journalist including others traveling to Middle Eastern countries. Therefore it becomes strange within how Americans can fight a war, and then the same people we just fought; certain executives and others sold them control of one of the most profitable, and dangerous Corporate American industry products that is offered in all regions.

Considering the fact that the Pentagon was attacked on September 11, 2001 a vast amount of U.S. military officials were victimized, and killed. This goes along the line of "Aiding An Enemy" especially during an American issue within "time of war". Observing this the American society became vulnerable, and not alert which means a certain amount of government, military officials, and civilians (c/o protecting even the Pentagon) were not doing a certain amount of things right. Then as this effected so many other Americans the government, and people found vital cause to get most government officials alert, and focused with appropriate involvement.

The defense of America, and occasionally other nations becomes a vital subject to control a responsible way for people to live. In the United States we consider this the common defense to promote domestic tranquility. Then prosperity is another part of this equation for Americans to live in a U.S. Constitutional way. Therefore American National Security, and the Commercial Airspace with all advancements in technology should be maintained in a logical, and law binding way of common values for the people to live free, safe, and in a natural way.

# SATELLITES WITH METAL, PHYSICAL, FINANCIAL, & FATAL HARM

(7)

## CHAPTER SEVEN

(7)

Anger and Technology In America

Worse Than The Watergate Crisis, Without Domestic Tranquility

# SATELLITES WITH METAL, PHYSICAL, FINANCIAL, & FATAL HARM

(7)

Commercial satellites moving from "Artificial Intelligence to General Intelligence" in the United States along with a few select foreign nations that are well developed have consisted of good, bad, and complex values of satellite technology. This was first established when America managed to create land based satellite technology, and then human space-flights with "satellite and orbital experiments". These experiments along with geological studies (c/o some defense values) in mind became progressive, and valued with technological advancements. This was valuable even as a distinct number of astronauts lost their lives in the pursuit of this level of American determination.

As dangerous space flight missions became scientific values of advancements, and studies which could be conducted between the plaint earth, and the outer orbits of space, various scientific disciplines were established. These were experiments which created satellite studies with good, and bad advancements of overall use. Then between the space missions of Mercury, Apollo, and the Challenger with the space shuttle instead of rockets, this became the establishment of orbital and land based corporate, and some individual satellite activity. These satellites were sent into the orbit of outer space which gave the American society a vast amount of new, and complex technology for a vast amount of useful social, business, and government disciplines.

Contrary to the Soviet Union in 1958 with the Sputnik satellite being first in outer space, the U.S. Mercury missions (c/o President John Kennedy) became valuable; then Americas space program began with expensive progress. This U.S.A. space program began with passion and advanced with seven astronauts, and resulted with one astronaut Deke Slayton being removed due to heart problems. These remaining Mercury mission astronauts in 1959 were Walter Schirra, John Glenn, Scott Carpenter, Alan Shepard, Gus Grissom, and Gordon Cooper.

After the Mercury mission's crew, another mission was Apollo which started, and consisted of Neil Armstrong, Michael Collins, and Buzz Aldrin whom accomplished the 1ˢᵗ moon walk in 1969. Then from there the Space Shuttle program, and other missions put an enormous amount of satellites into orbit. This was the work of numerous astronauts, engineers, and other professionals at NASA with these experimental program missions into orbit before it was reorganized or ended during the President Barack Obama administration.

A conditional amount of scientific achievements, and disciplines were established in outer space by astronauts for the operating standards of the National Oceanic Atmospheric Administration (NOAA) to determine advanced weather predictions, and water navigation priorities. Along with these achievements other values during the last Apollo mission by the National Aeronautics Space Administration (NASA) astronauts left behind a plaque on the moon that read: "Here Man completed his first exploration of the Moon, December 1972 A.D. May the spirit of peace in which we came be reflected in the lives of all mankind".

These words of "Mankind value" that were left on the moon in 1972 have been seriously taken out of content. This was done in a major capacity by instigated mental, physical, financial, and fatal harm. This becomes the logic with some satellite activity to be considered an Endless Loop Crisis. Then these occasionally instigated conflicts, and this even included an increase in certain types of violence. Considering this good, and bad technology awareness more Americans have committed tremendous crimes of violence (c/o people hearing voices), and financial crimes which have been extensive with technology. Therefore even the concept of madness within various people can cause heart attacks.

This mankind logic may even be a factual concern as some people don't acknowledge, and recognize these problems as maybe some doctors have, or even more so some scientist, and engineers have awareness. As doctors have not found a medical solution to the increasing medical problem of people hearing voices, conflicting anger and violence has been tremendous. Occasionally these somewhat inadmissible or un-affirmed disturbances have occurred from continued unregulated satellite activity with certain levels of destruction. Therefore, and otherwise these issues should have been considered with the collaboration of scientific and hopeful engineers with help from lawmakers.

Considering mankind and peace - anger with some people consist of being forced into bad retirement decisions, living standards, and diversified negligence which has pushed the American society backwards. This has become the good, and bad evaluation of certain established NASA, and or NOAA including certain other technology. The concept of this un-enforced regulated technology has been part of technological affirmations (lawfully), and even more so bad non-affirmative satellite activities. These technology disciplines then have overruled the U.S. Constitution with abused, and a weaker level of national security. Therefore a vast amount of NASA, NOAA, and National Security Administration (NSA) disciplines of law, various engineering, logical scientific-principals, and other concerns have somewhat caused a lack of domestic tranquility, and prosperity by numerous people that should not have had access.

Observing the good, and more so bad level of complexity within technology, numerous American citizens most times don't understand when satellite technology issues can be mentally, physically, financially, and sometimes fatally harmful, if not even manipulative. The concept and development of satellites have gotten to the point that lasers, unauthorized voice transitioning, or un-affirmed "voice transmissions" along with other conflicting technology must be outlined as safe and lawful use. These become issues which can occur just as NASA equipment can watch any landing far into outer space.

Sometimes considering various satellite technology it includes people full of hate with access that don't give up until some people or even some children's death. This becomes tragic and destructive unless they are prosecuted or Court Marshaled first. Then this even becomes a concern that all, or any levels of satellite technology can be economically destructive, or occasionally deadly to people when this satellite activity may overcome society with un-Constitutionally unlawful use. Observing this technology that is being used unlawfully, and or in a destructive capacity can cause tremendous harm. Otherwise this can be part of numerous American tragedies, similar "but" different to a nuclear explosion.

These satellite issues were also to be the developments of the NOAA, and NASA experiments. This also was a value which becomes the foundation for a vast amount of technological disciplines to appropriate logical work, and safety concerns to the American society. Between the NASA, and the logical work of NOAA conditional values have been part of creating, and evaluating natural issues that keep society safe, and efficient. This consideration becomes indifferent to most improvements, constitutional regulations, and U.S. policies for the use of various products supported within developments by NASA, and NOAA scientifically. Observing this these became judicial questions with the need of better oversight satellite technology concerns of lawful use. Therefore as these men (c/o some woman operators) from America putting satellite technology into a "land base, and more so an orbital" capacity, the transition of this activity was part of powerful technology concerns to be regulated.

Unregulated, or un-enforced regulatory issues have become the additional indifference of mental, physical, financial, and fatal concerns of harm when satellites are used illegally. This is 1 of about 5 major issues which created a tremendous factor within anger and technology in America. Therefore conflicting satellite regulation in various nations including America have been flawed, and un-enforced to keep Americans totally safe contrary to affirmed experiments.

Unlawful, and negligent satellite technology has taken disastrous, and unconstitutional advantage of most established Constitutional laws as well. The concept of orbital satellites observing Mankind with Peace and Tranquility has been damaged to an inadmissible capacity with numerous bad people becoming destructive, and or instigating violence. Sometimes this understanding even consist of violence without a clear motive except for unfairly or unlawful financial profits. These profits consist of anything that the courts can, or should understand, and or are unwilling to admit. Affirming this satellite problem is then part of various professionals that seem incapable to admit, or argue satellite crimes in a government official capacity which includes being heard in a logical court of law.

During the concept of human space-flights these missions were a dangerous process for some American astronauts that were somewhat competing against Russian cosmonaut advancements. Then their effort was to survive, and conduct experiments in orbit while they, and these experimental concerns consisted of them working safely. Contrary to this fact, then satellites along with products like bubble gun, water, and various types of food became complex in outer space with zero gravity. This was observed as more people became aware of the access to satellite communication illegally, then other people began hearing voices at record rates, and this caused destructive anger. Contrary to spy's this has been a level of "distraction socially" that keeps some American people from making clear decisions, and living a life of domestic tranquility with discipline.

Other concerns (c/o NASA evaluations from Doctors of Internal Medicine) at excessive rates was an experimental determination to be more cautious within the health dangers of astronauts or people in outer space. This is severely different from satellite, and orbital activity which a massive amount of people in America, and on the planet Earth would conditionally come to understand. Then this became the understanding and determination that even in outer-space special food, and other livable standards would become critically different with astronauts needing spacesuits and helmets. These issues in orbit consist of vitally different concerns apart from lawful living with scientific-principals on Earth. Therefore these issues were based on good, and bad research along with the development of "safe" products for astronauts to use, but not to cause harm, "in no illogical way" to the innocent people on Earth, and more so in America.

The American resource of commercial land based, and or orbital satellites is a technology that has been extensively complex. This format of technology developments has been progressive since the 1940s, the 1950s, and up throughout today within the first decades of the 2000s. Considering these decades of technology with good, and bad investments, some Americans have become complacent, and destructive by not observing logical regulation. These factors include conflicting crime which have become worse than the Watergate Crisis with internal American threats. Then these conflicting issues includes terrorist activity which has the potential to intensify, and cause different levels of harm to American's from international, and domestic spy's.

Observing the U.S. Space Shuttle program more satellites were sent, and positioned in outer space than any time in American space history. This became important with critical values of technology that still need to be regulated just like the times during the 1920s as it applies to economic disciplines for numerous business, and banking industry concerns. Therefore even as various banking institutions (c/o investment or commerce banks) are using this technology, they also must comply with laws, and the U.S. Constitution.

As those decades within times have changed, the millennium years of 2000 with new challenges, and experiments have become critical to evaluate the vital need of satellite technology affirmations, and government regulation. These issues have conditional results, and achievements which are diversified within technology that hold good, and bad resources of industry concerns effecting all Americans. Even some "computer, and satellite banking services" have been part of major losses (c/o hundreds of millions or billions of dollars) for an enormous amount of American investors, depositors, and consumers.

Observing values that consist of satellite technology which is more out-of-reach then normal, a valued understanding to most Americans is conflicting to the society that we live in. Then as we can be "Seen From Far-Away" distance's, and be "Heard From Far-Away" distance's; these communication spectrum resources have overruled some long-term U.S. Constitutional standards. Most of these standards are within law, technology, engineering, and scientific-principals to think about maintaining the health, financial, and domestic tranquility of American citizens. Therefore this format of technology is not the most destructive, but it is one of the highest matters of lawful regulatory concerns.

In America it is not uncommon that certain technology observed in the United States as corporate products on occasions become a dangerous problem. Contrary to the Manhattan Project within nuclear weapons, numerous medications, automobiles, and other products that did not work properly had to be recalled. These are revisions and legal court matters with government hearings on various products which became valued for corrections throughout the American society, and the courts. Then this has established a valuable consideration of what products lawfully work, and what products don't work in a safe, and efficient way.

As we in America observe conflicting products, commercial satellites is one product (c/o thousands of systems covering millions of people) that consist of many mysterious operating conditions. These are resourceful products that have good, and bad values effecting law, and scientific-principals. Even as we have observed the results of the Atom bomb on Hiroshima, and Nagasaki, Japan in World War II it consisted of a long term disaster. These long term issues of disaster were determined in a humanity issue of environmental lifetime radioactive harm. This was a capacity of radiation that "no" human, and or even animals could survive. Understanding this, various satellite activity that is unregulated without enforcement can be just as harmful to almost any values of normal life existence.

Considering these facts in America a tremendous amount commercial satellite technology, and other future products have to be considered in a discrete and productive way within use. Even the use of the internet has been a factor to manipulate, and instigate a level of suicide, murder, financial fraud, and other crimes. Then contrary to the internet, commercial satellites with no affirmation leaves people confused with instigated conflicts that sometimes turn violent.

As violent and instigated conflicts have reached disturbing levels, American communities are occasionally suffering from the 1st and 4th Amendments of the Constitution. The most disturbing factors are the loss in productive families, marriages, and people that could help the economy, and various issues of moral support throughout the American society. These are values that them and others could have lawfully provided to a vast amount of other American citizens to manage domestic tranquility. Also the different establishments of religion can endure problems of how moral Freedom of Religion (c/o also Speech) values within worship can be disturbed without logical affirmation. Then these U.S. Constitutional law or regulatory standards, and scientific principal violations of unobserved law enforcement have become a part of a self-destructive American society.

The concept of social self-destruction with illegal and hazardous commercial satellites being mentally, physically, financially, and fatally harmful has enormous problems at diversified record rates. Observing at least 6 people that committed tremendous acts of violence with unclear motives was Adam Lanza (c/o Sandy Hook), Aaron Alexis (c/o the Washington D.C Navy Yard), Andrea Yates (c/o Houston, Texas), Magdalena Lopez (Dyer, Indiana), Angelica Alvarez (c/o Elkhart County, Indiana), Kevin Isom (c/o Gary, Indiana), and there was a vast amount of others. As these people seem to suffer mentally it should be reminded that their actions were part of a historical level of anger.

Adam Lanza was a young man whom seem to suffer mentally for years even as myself and others recognized over most of his 20 years of life that illegal and hazardous commercial satellite use (c/o 1990 to 2010 plus) had been completely out of control in numerous other regions. Then on December 14, 2014 Adam Lanza turned rational on the American society at Sandy Hook Elementary School as he shot and killed 27 children, and adults with 2 other people injured. His motive is still unclear as he killed himself which no prosecutor has anything of logic to argue as of yet in the courts whether he was bullied before or artificial intelligence caused him to have homicidal thoughts. Considering this tragedy in the State of Connecticut miles away from the elementary school he killed his mother Nancy Lanza before his rampage which means that an enormous amount of anger, and distraction with conflicts overcame this "angry" young man.

Aaron Alexis during September 16, 2013 went on a rampage of killing at a U.S. Naval Yard in Washington D.C. as he was working for a contractor at this U.S. Naval facility. He was considered a fair to nice guy, but occasionally with a temper that became hard to control. One major factor is that he complained of hearing voices (c/o extremely low frequency electromagnetic waves) which I consider Illegal and Hazardous Commercial Satellite use or part of artificial intelligence. This seems to have led to continued and increased anger, which caused him to go on a killing spree of a vast amount of somewhat, and mostly innocent people. Aaron Alexis shot and killed 12 people, with 3 others left injured. This occurred before he was shot and killed by a responding officer upon which his rampage lasted "1 hour and about 9 minutes" with excessive gunfire.

Magdalena Lopez was a mother in the northwest Indiana Town of Dyer whom killed her 2 sons with a "10 pound barbell weight" causing fatal blunt force trauma. She clam's that (c/o a considered bipolar disorder) she explains her mental stability was being ripped apart piece by piece. Therefore Magdalena Lopez felt that she could no longer care for her two adolescent sons Antonio 9, and Erik 2 years old. In August of 2009 she was sentenced to 110 years in prison. Then this basically seems to be consistent with a number of other unpredictable people, and her; whom were confused about what truly provoked this level of anger and violence against her most innocent love ones.

Kevin Isom (c/o the Miller section of Gary, In) shot and killed his wife Cassandra Isom, and his 2 stepchildren Michael Moore 16, and Ci'Andria Cole at 13 years old. This tragic event occurred on August 8, 2007 which was during a time in Gary, Indiana that consisted of illegal and hazardous commercial satellites being used, and completely out of control. This was an unformatted level of activities that seems to have increased domestic murder, and even infant mortality which occurred at highly conflicting rates.

Kevin Isom an unemployed security guard by trade, was in a mentally delusive mine state once the Gary Police Department officers arrested him. His main statement is that: I can't believe I killed my family! This level of terror possibly for the victims, and conditionally for the suspect must have been a tremendous ordeal considering the intent if he really meant to do what he done, or did some other "person or issue" (c/o commercial satellites) instigate this tragedy. Even if others instigated or provoked this tragedy with intent or negligence the overall consolidated factor of damage, and violence was severely wrong and becomes complex with punishable factors, and vital to correct especially for future concerns.

Angelica Alvarez (c/o Elkhart County, In) was 27 years old when she killed her 4 young children on the day of November 14, 2006. Their names, and ages were Jennifer Lopez 8, Gonzalo Lopez Jr. 6, Daniel Valdez 4, and

Jessica Valdez 2 which altogether was classified as a "domestic" mass murder. As this situation may have been slightly a mental level of exhaustion, and or an aggravated mental level of distraction with disturbances, the prosecution observed that her like some others whom were "nonviolent and then turned violent" is a mysterious, and complex problem.

A father of 2 of Angelica Alvarez's children Gonzalo Lopez Sr. said through a translator that he forgives her, and the prosecutor Curtis Hill outlined; that this did not have to happen, but her spending the rest of her life in jail now dose. Then as she had left a note about what she had done (contrary to mental health evaluations & treatment), her "decision making had diminished". Therefore she worried about a brake up, and or divorce from her husband that implemented tremendous grief, and intimidation that she could no longer take care of her children, so she strangled them to death.

Andrea Yates (c/o Houston, Texas) whom killed her 5 young children on June 20, 2001 in a bathtub by drowning them to death, has been part of many medical evaluations, and trial court conflicts. She confessed to committing this violent crime with unclear motives, and then was tried again due to the insecurity of an expert medical witness. Her life before this terrible act was observed when Andrea Yates was in high school, and she graduated valedictorian in 1982 while also being captain of the swimming team at Milby High School in Texas. Then as a professional she became a registered nurse in the medical industry which followed a prosperous childhood growing up with a good education. Andrea Yates did suffer numerous mental brake-downs before this violent act which some people observed her as somewhat a religious zealot.

Contrary to Andrea Yates having a good upcoming, with logical parents, and her NASA engineer husband whom had commitments to his job, they also shard a logic that they as a married couple wanted as many children as possible. As their ambition of having a large family consisted of conflicting issues, her condition like some others continued to change for the worse. Then if satellite technology was a factor it seems that this was a long-term course of action which has occurred similar to some other people. Observing this a vast amount of these other people within a violent state of concern had opportunities, but not much support, educational awareness, or their on manageable guidance. This mostly left them in a dark hole, or being guided by something that was more so unlawfully powerful, and more destructive then they could tolerate, or mentally handle.

As the American Medical Association, and the Medical industry throughout America is appropriately active, other issues of different professional, and product values have been created. These professions and products are similar, and different with advancements to those of the pass. This is observed considering now microscopic radiology, pathology, robotics, and chemical experiments have been part of advanced resources of technology. A troubling part of this consist of negligence within technological use with certain products, and procedures which includes careless, bad, or unqualified people with dangerous technology access. Then this should become part of vital government issues which consist of a relevant evaluation for the liability conditions that the people may endure.

Understanding men and woman that are subjected to any mental, physical, financial, and or fatal satellite or other technology harm this takes tremendous government evaluations and procedures to correct. Then as this issue (c/o the millennium years of 2000) is somewhat similar, and worse than the Watergate crisis and hearings of 1972, and 1973 the American system of justice (c/o lawyers and other professionals) has issues of adjustable products, and secured liability issues to argue. Also this includes other legislature within regulatory agencies, and commissions in government which must adapt to these changing times. These professions of medicine and health, engineering with wireless communication and others with similar Constitutional, and law arguments including regulatory enforcement disciplines should keep the people from becoming abused by danger or damage.

Observing the physical harm that illegal and hazardous commercial satellites can possibly cause consist of complex internal health problems sometimes due to anger. These are physical health problems like heart attacks, increasingly dangerous blood pressure, and other exerted, or illness factors with sometimes discretionary cures. Satellites that have computers, and lazars with operational connections can cause exerted exhaustion which considering a weak persons heart rate, and blood flow can cause cardiovascular disorders, and clogged arteries. These are issues similar to aggressive activities that lead to heart failure, stroke, aneurysm, and or heart attacks.

Various physical conditions, and professional activities are similar to complex procedures of how lazars are used carefully in "medical operations of surgery". The American professional difference with these technological activities consist of the medical operation disciplines within surgery by the use of lazar extractions that are conducted by a licensed physician.

Understanding these are doctors of internal medicine in hospitals, this most times provide directions, affirmations, and occasional signed agreements for these procedures. Considering this level of effort they then consist of highly trustworthy medical affirmations of discipline, and a professional health care format within security.

On the other side of this comparison of illegal and hazardous commercial satellite use strong laser and satellite vibrations that can penetrate the human anatomy, and cause damage to internal organs is a problem. This problem which if done by people seeking to cause harm can instigate or produce unlawfully negative results. This has even been reviewed by secured experiments within the U.S. Department of Defense with what is considered as a shock waving electrical invisible fence.

This "electrical invisible fence" product is not publicly used due to the un-affirmed "Danger & Warning Signs" within liability of the product, and technology. Then it is important to understand that electrical fence technology that is not invisible has been around for over 5 decades, but now advancements have been made. Therefore as criminals do not always warn or affirm people of danger, others providing lawful enforcement, responsibilities of high security government facilities, and the heavy equipment industry most times having a legal discipline within affirmed danger. This affirmed awareness within liabilities can consist of dangerous facilities, equipment, and chemicals to warn anybody of the general public of this dangerous property, airspace, and or certain manufacturing or construction job site activities.

Evaluating unlawful commercial satellite physical harm, numerous Americans like Michael J. Fox whom have been diagnosed with rare disorders such as Parkinson disease which in his case a cure is in the mist of extensive research. As a cure for this disease has not been established this becomes another "possible satellite" level of "possible" physical harm. Other illnesses, and diseases that I consider should be observed are aneurysm, and certain forms of cancer. Contrary to the fact some people have found medications, and productive treatment, but these complex diseases and negative conditions of illness are similar to anything that can make the human anatomy suffer strange reactions.

Considering these tremendously important subjects of satellites with mental, physical, financial, and fatal harm in America, some state and federal laws being enforced have been the failure of complacent, and insecure government. This becomes the observation that a vast amount of officials will say that's impossible, but we did seem to put men on the moon. Observing these technology advancements with their every step on the moon, and creating other technology like robots that can make peanut butter and jelly sandwiches or make some repairs and or build cars the American industry times have changed.

As cars, and so many other manufacturing processes, and scientific issues within smaller computers "that now" store more memory has changed the American society we live in as this made most "artificial intelligence transition into general intelligence". Then we must still take note of the most normal way humans live, and even with new or existing Constitutional laws how it applies to these good, occasionally bad, and complex issues of technology.

# THE FEDERAL COMMUNICATION COMMISSION WITH STATUTE OF LIMITATIONS
(8)

## CHAPTER EIGHT
(8)

Anger and Technology In America

Worse Than The Watergate Crisis, Without Domestic Tranquility

# THE FEDERAL COMMUNICATION COMMISSION WITH STATUTE OF LIMITATIONS

(8)

During the last 3 decades (c/o the 1980s, 1990s, and 2000s) anger in the United States has continued to increase along with Americas technological communication advancements. Upon this concern vital issues include various regulated disciplines that seem to be slightly or sometimes inadequate. These are good, and bad values within television, radio, telephone with telecommunication systems, and even satellite broadcasting that is regulated by the Federal Communication Commission. Therefore with additional technology expansions that includes "bands and bandwidths" of frequencies the American system of state and federal government must be factual with enforcement. Then they must proceed with the uttermost of regulation, legislature, and better or logical enforcement for these complex systems.

In various times certain satellite broadcasting, which may include other lawful, and or more so unlawful activities have become worse than the Watergate crisis. Also this is a factor in other strange acts of deception, anger, and instigated violence. Although America has had centuries of crime, conflict, and violent acts including war, these recent decades have consisted of financial crime matters, mass murders, domestic murders, and tremendous harm against more innocent people taking parts of the United States backwards. These important people include more children than in any other historical time in America.

Between the Richard Nixon and Barack Obama U.S. Presidential administration's a vast amount of low level and high level amateur, professional, licensed, and unlicensed people have created good and some bad communication technology conflicts. These where conflicts within telecommunication, and communication systems (c/o even the internet) which have conditionally taken control of various regions, and markets. Understanding these issues throughout the American society in a more so destructive way has been the observation of when we have recognized extreme violence, or financial harm.

Considering American communities and satellite technology the observation of decades after the Watergate crisis, and hearings have accumulated more destructive people to use unlawful satellite technology. These are people whom seem to what to use those unlawful communication or spy activities with more advanced equipment. Then these unlicensed operators with technical violations of law have created a way with advanced technology to "receive, obtain, or transmit" information illegally, and to instigate diversified harm, or destructive attributes. These critically harmful concerns, therefore become vital issues of the Federal Communication Commission (FCC), and others in government whom seem to have or instigated a cause to act without evaluations, logical enforcement, and legislative disciplines.

The Federal Communication Commission also has a duty to enforce regulation in the jurisdiction of commercial airways, airspace, and the overall capacity of millions of operational transmitters in the communication industry. These systems occasionally have more so become advanced levels of technological activities, and occasional crime. Then this is a concern, and issue for government to control our Constitutional capacity of livable standards. Considering these facts, this makes U.S. Constitutional laws, and more so the Statute of Limitations along with regulatory standards complex, and partly failing issues in a variation of ways when enforcement is obsolete.

The concept, and condition of people hearing voices before they commit severely violent acts of crime is part of an expanded "commercial satellite and airspace" problem which can also be violations of Executive Orders of law. Even the existing U.S. President can not violate "past and or future" Executive Orders of law without approved consent from the legislature or judicial branches of government; unless authorized by reason of his Chief Commanding duties. Then the length of time it takes to correct these occasionally complex resources of law, and critical problems through the courts with expenses is the good and bad of what looks to now be a failing condition of limited law, and social standards of disaster.

As logical laws, specifications, and standards apply to numerous parts of the American society of citizen or victim awareness, knowledge of what to do, and government enforcement becomes vital. So as these issues sometimes instigate other problems for maybe millions of people, and the Constitutions "domestic tranquility" the American people can and has endured suffering. Therefore domestic tranquility, prosperity, and the Statute of Limitations along with the Limitations of Liability Act becomes important arguments with ethical disciplines.

A Black's Law dictionary provides the definitions of "Statute of Limitations", and the Limitations of Liability Act as follows. The Statute of Limitations: is statute of the federal government and various states setting maximum time periods during which certain actions can be brought "to justice" (c/o government) or rights enforced. After the time period set out in the applicable statute of limitations has run, no legal action can be brought regardless of whether any cause of action ever existed. Also: a statute prescribing limitations to the right of action on certain described causes of action or criminal prosecution; that is, declaring that no suit, shall be maintained on such causes of action, nor any criminal charge be made, unless brought within a specified period of time after the right accrued (as this applies to statutes of limitation for actions against the U.S. government). Otherwise in criminal cases, however, a statute of limitation is an act of grace, and a surrendering by sovereignty of its rights to prosecute.

The other Black's Law dictionary describes the Limitation of Liability acts as: state and federal statutes that limit liability for certain types of damage (e.g., pain and suffering) or limited liability of certain persons or groups (e.g., liability of corporate directors for acts of corporations), or limit time period in which action can be maintained (c/o Statute of Limitations). Other subjects follow such as Caps, Federal Tort Claims Act, Sovereign Immunity, and No Fault.

These Limitation of Liability acts within law recently have been part of legal actions. This diversified format of problems is observed with concern for "the (2010) BP Deepwater Horizon accident and oil spill", the (2005) Texas City, Texas explosion (c/o BP accidents) and other "Corporate" incidents or discretionary disasters. This 2010 "Louisiana" fatal accident created a bill in the Senate of the U.S. Congress as "the Deepwater Horizon Survivors Fairness Act. Then as it applies to the Parliament of the United Kingdom (c/o England, Wales, Scotland, and Northern Ireland) similar laws and legal action have occurred. These issues within the Limited Liability Act (1855 & Present) have more than likely been observed within the law case of the "News of The World" newspaper (c/o Rupert Murdoch with other bad corporate officials) as a corporate phone hacking scandal.

Various U.S. Constitutional issues are facts which includes how numerous industries are regulated, and contrary to anger which may include violence, this is partly how the advanced need of regulatory solutions will be hopeful priorities of legislatively established laws. Some of these harmful acts are the result of unethical disagreements, protecting property, or even self-defense. Observing domestic or massive conflicting murders some suspects or defendants barely can give a valid or logical motive for the tragic act they committed, if they live. This becomes important within the governments logic of regulation, and affirmed state and federal Statute of Limitations to control enforcement of certain technological activities "outside and inside" of the courts for the innocence of American people.

Understanding the consideration of any government or corporate officials that uses satellites, radar, wire taps, or any technology illegally or unlawfully against people (contrary to a direct crime) of the United States or local businesses is a severe problem the courts "should not" ignore. This becomes an enormous problem that lately may include more so "supporting an enemy foreign agenda". Then these American established businesses working to survive or expand contrary to government officials that act as bullies should not have immunity for, or during any legal actions. These are facts to observe that a vast amount of American born citizens sacrificed, and worked hard to create a workable concept of businesses. Those businesses usually consisted of a format within operating resources of income earnings of discipline and being helpful to the people.

Considering government immunity this includes all executive, legislative, judicial, or professional government offices like within prosecutors, lawyers, treasures, assessors, surveyors, engineers, or associates similar to, and including the U.S. Geological Survey with others. Understanding this the concept of a majority of the American system of government can't be understood completely for these subjects without discretionary legal matters, and responsible politics. Americans observe a logical definition of "politics" as: the science of government; the art of practice within administering public affairs as it applies to most and all levels of government. Ultimately this becomes a careful process between government, and even the highest level of professionalism.

A vast amount of conflicts became critical during the tenure of Bruce Babbitt the former governor of Arizona as he became Secretary of the Department of Interior with the FCC, the U.S. Geological Survey (c/o geosynchronous and or geostationary satellites) under their jurisdiction. Contrary to the U.S. Geological Survey consisting of satellite capabilities and activities during the 1990s, this became part of these times in America which a vast amount of young citizens loss positive societal control. This control was the destructive concern to gang violence in the streets of America. Then other people were victimized in diversified, and conflicting ways which was part of many crisis concerns. Therefore as it applies to the Federal Communication Commission a vast amount victimized citizens can be easily confused about any conflicting violations of American law, and discretionary government values.

So as these times during the 1990s which included William Daly, and others a vast amount of tragic acts struck innocent Americans in many ways. Some of these tragic acts they recognized and some they severely did not. This included some of the most historic industry fatal accidents (c/o Texas City, Texas, Northwest Indiana, and Milwaukee, Wisconsin with other states), and acts of crime or tragic negligence. Then this also included terrorism (c/o the 9-11 Report and the U.S. Department of Defense) which dramatically changed parts of our American society with alerts, and security details.

Contrary to terrorism BP's Texas City, Texas (2005) explosion occurred 5 years before the BP Deepwater Horizon explosion, and severe oil leak in the Gulf of Mexico and New Orleans. Surrounding this issue during 1996 Bata Steel had a massive explosion in Portage, Indiana which defies the evidence for any Statute of Limitations. This observation also included the 2006 Falk Corporation in Milwaukee which consisted of a fatal explosion with a few fatalities, and massive injuries that was part of an Endless Loop of destruction. Then this became the logic that some format of technology is not being used properly for productive business that is completely safe for American workers.

As technology changes, and more Americans occasionally here voices in the "commercial or residential" airspace -- more fatal manufacturing accidents have seem to occur. This is not a normal issue for the Federal Communication Commission or even the Environmental Protection Agency, but people with communication values that penetrate the environments natural conditions have been effected with a strong lack of sovereignty. Then this insecurity becomes a similar concern for a "U.S. or Individual State" Special Prosecutor similar to the Watergate Legal Hearings with the appointment of Special Prosecutor - Archibald Cox.

The observation of the U.S. Constitution and FCC laws includes good, bad, conflicting and or complex government surveillance along with communication, television, radio, and satellite "stations for broadcasting", air traffic control, and national security. This also includes phone companies and other large corporate businesses with access that becomes extremely indifferent contrary to normal business, to the American society. Therefore now with more satellites and various internet activities these issues include new Federal Communication Commission resources with challenges. These are communication challenges due to numerous advancements during this information technology level of expansion with products, and active uses of legal discipline.

Over the years since the early 1990s millions of people have found various FCC regulated technology which is important for business, and social disciplines of livable standards. This is the logic that most public, private, small and large businesses and corporations have web-sites and other technology that promotes their business values. As the United Nations includes over 160 other nations that are developed with this tragedy, the FCC only requires most communication companies to register with them. Then Germany, Russia, China, Japan, India, Italy, Canada, Mexico, Africa, Cuba, and a few other major countries operating in America must observe FCC regulations which have a logical governed level of affirmations. Therefore to regulate these international technology concerns, a disciplined level of affirmations are understood as vital.

Some of these FCC issues are part of the liberties of Americans as it applies to the U.S. federal government which has been debated within new and existing laws. These are considered the good, and bad of law issues like the Patriot Act or the Anti-Terrorism Act of 2001 which became conditionally valuable after the 9-11 Report attacks. This concept of laws becomes the resource within adjusting legal disciplines that apply to communication, and the people's rights of privacy, confidentiality, and solitude. Otherwise as the American (state & federal) system of government seeks to find terrorist, dangerous criminals internationally, and more so domestically in America these laws should not destroy innocent American citizens.

Considering the FCC and the U.S. federal government's effort during the George Bush Jr. administration, and the September 11, 2001 attacks numerous precautions were taken before, and during a war time discipline. Observing the Patriot Act and or the Anti-Terrorism Act of 2001 back in the early 1990s some of the same issues of obtaining information "with or without" a warrant occurred. Understanding this becomes the observation that good, bad, and conflicting businesses including government satellites for communication issues have occurred (c/o not preventing the 9-11 Report terrorist attacks). Then this has also taken certain born in American citizens (c/o even more so black Americans) backwards as it applies to mental, and financial American values.

As U.S. domestic issues intervene, or are manipulated to the extent of National Security some people have found destructive uses of various technology against certain local citizens. The lawful and legislative intent for these issues of security (c/o the Patriot Act and the Anti-Terrorism Act) also conflicted with the Foreign Intelligence Surveillance Act which made it occasionally a difficult and slow process to get a warrant "even" from the courts as a U.S. Department of Defense General. This was observed by Air Force General Mike Hayden of the George Bush Jr. administration to track the activities of the Taliban, and al Qaeda operatives, contrary to vitally finding Osama bin Laden.

Understanding the insecurity of some American businesspeople or people with conflicts these issued law and technology concerns become their way of trying to make progress or "take advantage" of discretionary social, business, or government resources. Then if you compare these factors to the Watergate scandal considering over 40 years ago some Americans that want to be "quiet dictators" or "criminals:" have taken certain parts of the American society backwards in the likes of at least 85 years. Observing the U.S. Department of Justice, and the Congress any action of Watergate types of eavesdropping is serious especially compared to foreign enemies like al Qaeda. This became security matters that had to be reassigned, and reappointed against dangerous enemies. Then this had become a practice with hardly no law court affirmations that harms innocent American citizens at record rates.

Americans at record rates have been harm with the indirect but destructive likes of William Daly (Chicago) and Karen F. Wilson of Gary (c/o government, business, and other unorganized resources) which became disastrous. This was closely connected and or them being addicted to illegally obtaining information, and transmitting destructive information that became disastrous in many ways. Then this became tremendously overcome by gang violence against small business owners and conflicting or innocent people.

As this became what is considered White Collar or Technology Cloud crimes observing the 1980s to 2015 as communication systems became more of a factor within unlawful technology -- dictatorships appeared. These factors even with good, and more so complex business agreements consisting of excellent technology was an arbitrary condition within telecommunication and communication resourceful systems. Therefore this has taken a majority of the American society full speeds backwards upon which government has even made mistakes or committed crimes.

Observing these issues of unlawful insecurity the concept of Americans supporting certain enemy foreign agendas was evident with the September 11, 2001 attacks, and other conflicts. As some citizens made an attempt to offer any kind of "WARNING" of terrorist activity -- these Americans were the last people to be listened too. Therefore local government is places like Gary, Indiana and Chicago, Illinois instigated people to be incompetent or stupid until tragedy struck. Then most other issues in all forms of American government allowed terrorist to kill as many Americans as possible.

Contrary to American government and major corporations (c/o even AT&T or Ameritech) not helping to prevent the 9-11 Report Attacks other discretionary disasters continued to occur. This was the inefficient activity of close to 3,000 American people dying in Pennsylvania, Washington D.C., New York (c/o September 11, 2001), and more than 2,000 American people dying during Hurricane Katrina in 2005. Otherwise the tremendous issue of the FCC, with the courts and the Statutes of Limitation was not helpful which included a vast amount of people that suffered without legal compensation apart from the victims of these tragic acts, and some insecure issues of government in America.

# COMMERCIAL SATELLITE TECHNOLOGY (FOREIGN & U.S. DOMESTIC)

(9)

# CHAPTER NINE

(9)

Anger and Technology In America

Worse Than The Watergate Crisis, Without Domestic Tranquility

# COMMERCIAL SATELLITE TECHNOLOGY (FOREIGN & U.S. DOMESTIC)

(9)

The concept of U.S. Domestic and Foreign Satellites that are active in most all commercial airspace has been a factual advancement of many forms of technology in America and internationally. As it applies to residential and commercial airspace with satellites stationed on earth and in orbit, the understanding of transitions becomes complex. The complexity is a serious issue due to tracking or evaluating a lawful, or unlawful capacity of satellite activity, and humane discipline.

Observing the good, and bad within commercial satellites has occasionally consisted of factors that have conditional ways of satellite systems causing a lack of full sovereignty. Understanding this level of sovereignty which causes a loss in wealth, and prosperous opportunities is critical. This means they are being used, and are part of experimentation with additional subjects like geology, laser technology, and even financial matters (c/o the economy) and other subjects. Then as it applies to good, and bad laws the legislative, and more so the Judicial branch of American government have vital duties to correct these opinionated or diversified issues. Otherwise along with the Constitution of the United States, there is constant adjustments, and regulatory issues of enforcement that are vital.

Considering the first satellite was placed into the outer-space of orbit was named Sputnik from Russian government cosmonauts, and scientist this gave the United States very serious concerns about overall national security. This becomes part of bad national security that consist of various conditions of possible anger upon protecting America. So as these became Russian and international orbital space activities as it applies to the observation of the 1960's with the U.S. President John F. Kennedy and his administration, technology took on new, and diversified advancements. Then this outlines the good, bad, lawful, and unlawful achievements of satellite use from these international experiments, and developments with technological products.

Also during the 1960s this became the "Race for the Moon" and other diversified space travel with research, development, and experiments. Contrary to these international experiments Americans have only slightly considered if any conditions of this technology is used in a "Mixture" to be Constitutionally unlawful or maybe even lawful in America against the people. This is where we in America have observed a tremendous increase in anger and new or an arbitrational resource of important or vital technological products. Therefore this becomes the logic of good and bad technology within foreign relations with the determination of lawful, safe, and the domestic tranquility within use of commercial satellite systems.

The level of most space travel with various forms of technology existed between the United States, and other international scientific communities and constituents. These were constituents and countries like Germany, Russia, Japan, England, and a few others with concerns of satellite technology between the planet earth, and orbit. Otherwise this also became part of expended telecommunication and communication systems with large corporate systems funded by large corporate and or government investments. Then as it applies to small or large undeveloped countries on occasion this became part of international investments with occasional international terrorism.

As large corporations do business worldwide, this was observed during the John F. Kennedy presidential administration up throughout today with the administrations of President George Bush Jr., and President Barack Obama. Also the National Security Administration, the Federal Communication Commission, the Federal Trade Commission, and other U.S. government concerns have allowed these factors of "international investments and international terrorist" to destroy the domestic tranquility of an enormous amount of citizens in the United States. Contrary to this fact most major American corporations that operate internationally are occasionally part of these issues, but they do try to have workable agreements with the U.S. government especially for national security. Then similar to victimized airline companies on September 11, 2001 vital government measures had to be considered and taken into concern with the establishment of the U.S. Department of Homeland Security.

The level of vital concern for American domestic tranquility consist of normal and safe prosperity for the people, various occupations, and numerous professionals. Some of the most beneficial professions are meteorology, and engineering within how Hurricane Katrina effected the infrastructure of New Orleans, Louisiana during 2005. Also this became a severe issue of tragedies in other parts of America whom suffered some of Americas worse historical disasters applied to floods, and other infrastructure discrepancies. Considering these facts of historical destruction, and even the financial frustration that the people endured has given the American society Unconstitutional circumstances that must consist of a better social format in the future years to come.

Considering the corrections, or revisions of these satellite technological issues, and sometimes disastrous facts within the American society, we have a need to live in a safe, profitable, and prosperous society. This becomes the societal format of environmental and social discipline with lawful technology that is suppose, to be helpful, but "It Did Not" prevent the 9-11 terrorist attacks, and the overall storm-water damage of hurricane's Katrina and Ike. Hurricane Katrina (2005) and hurricane Ike (2008) caused an enormous amount of damage (c/o an obsolete infrastructure) to various regions of America including New Orleans. Contrary to the hurricane being predicted, this disastrous problem made hundreds of thousands of American people angry, and financially frustrated with restructuring their way of life to live by all government standards.

As American government standards have somewhat improved for the people, and business to maintain safe food, safe workplaces, safe households, and livable standards some conditions and facilities have hit rock bottom. These conditions of inadequate standards are due to sometimes the use of "illegal and hazardous commercial satellites", and other crimes which have destroyed thousands of residential, and business assets and establishments. This part of people not being able to make good decisions just as Detroit accumulated 78,000 abandon properties is a Looping Crisis in numerous cities throughout America.

Various American issues includes those people in Detroit, Michigan Gary, Indiana Harrisburg, Pennsylvania, and other American cities. These facts also include gang violence, with a level of unlawful technology that has created a large equation of destructive or domestic violence, destructive criminal acts with no motives, and unemployment. Otherwise this has become the diversion of how black American cities may have been victimized similar to a few white American towns or cities. Then this observation became the discrepancy of men and woman whom have been coerced to kill their families, various children, or to commit mass murders which may include suicide.

An unconditional issue in Black America became different when black professionals in the American society did not work lawfully with the good, and bad of commercial satellites. Then those black Americans, became destructive similar to white Americans who did not sometimes care about the logic of good, and bad foreign relations and American domestic tranquility. Otherwise these U.S. domestic concerns with international issues of conflict has seem to penetrate the American society with historical disasters.

Contrary to President Richard Nixon and the Watergate scandal these issues of bad foreign relations continued to get worse. Those bad issues within people like Slobodan Milosevic (Serbia), Saddam Hussein, Osama bin Laden (the Middle East), Manual Noriega (Panama) Jean-Paul Akayesu (Taba), Fonday Sankoh (Sierra Leona), Charles Taylor (Liberia) and others became part of international tragedies. This was part of their involvement in worldwide regional mutilation of the limes of young people, other violent crimes, and civil unrest. Therefore this became parallel to some of the most terrorizing tragic acts to America, and more so to international communities we as Americans try to understand through the American system of government, and the United Nations.

When certain levels of destructive events became bad to America the Constitution of individual states, and the United States slightly consisted of unlivable standards for various people. This occurred between 1990 and throughout 2010, but with 3 out 1,000 of the worse tragedies occurring on September 11, 2001, the Oklahoma City bombing, and Hurricane Katrina in part with various killings at schools as the American society fell weak, incompetent, or insecure to various issues. Then this was also a factor as various American manufacturing facilities became idled to fatal explosions with extreme negligence. In part to fatal explosions - infant mortality, domestic murder suicide, and even mass shootings of killing children, and other people; this became a crisis of increasing problems of social justice, and a lack of domestic tranquility which is similar to undeveloped countries.

Domestic tranquility in America has now taken this turn of being insecure, and part of passive religious and criminal indifference, which is bad, and or very complex. These become the facts with most religious congregations that explain that those fatal victims are in a better place (c/o heaven or hell) apart from living in the American society which was a misguided factor that got worse. This could be were too many people (c/o the youth), and government officials did not find a solution other than jail or prison for the recent increase of illogical violence, and even fatal negligence. Therefore an Endless Loop Crisis has been fully part of extracting as many Americans as quietly as possible with nothing but excuses other than illogical ignorance or indifference from some members of the clergy, and some government officials, otherwise ignoring a crisis.

Heaven and Hell - as it applies to religion has never been considered so indifferent between young and old Americans. Observing this fact young people killing each other and or going to jail or prison for long periods of time has extremely given enormous amounts of foreign people an extensive level of opportunities to establish business, and find prosperity that Americans were guaranteed. Considering these facts some of the lawful disciplines of the U.S. Constitution's Preamble occasionally needs to be argued good enough to keep America from some enormous steps backwards, which has become a critical factor.Otherwise with more immigrants coming to America it seems there is less people concerned about the U.S. Constitution, and how it establishes us as Americans with an unstable society of lawful integrity.

America being different from other developed and undeveloped nations has been a sign of logical government resources that is part of productive industry standards. On a vast amount of occasions this becomes the issue of if certain products are being used safely and without being part of destructive crime. This has been the case with some issues of television, radio, satellites, and the internet as it applies to fraud, indecency, and other distractions of harmful crime, various fatal acts, and or negligence. Then a prefect example is how a police car engaged in an automobile chase ends up as someone's tragic death which was filmed, and televised. This has happened nationally numerous times in the late 1990s, and early 2000s crating a sad level of respect for the person or people that are killed, and even the family of the deceased.

Contrary to crime and negligence television, radio, satellites, and the internet have made good, bad, and complex advancements. So it is not to say these are not valuable resources of technological products, services, and systems, but government enforcement for lawful use is a vital standard to maintain. Another relevant fact is that television and radio like newspapers will print or announce that they made an error, or mistake with corrections to large amounts of people. Then as it applies to mistakes, errors, or the need of a correction within negligent commercial satellite use - "is or has" this ever legally been affirmed? Even if it provokes the killing of children - has government, prosecutors or expert witnesses been able to affirmed this conflicting problem?

The United States and some other developed countries like Russia, France, Germany, parts of Africa, and the United Kingdom (c/o England) have created a vast amount of positive uses for commercial satellites, but most of these countries have still been victimized by terrorist attacks, and daily problems. These terrorist from enemy countries or certain regions of the world like Iraq, Afghanistan, Yemen, and a few others have had a vast amount of people whom have used satellite technology, and the internet in good and conditionally disturbing ways along with Americans. Therefore our foreign and U.S. domestic level of technology becomes a concern that requires proper legislative corrections.

Mexico with their recent President Enrique Nieto having satellite capabilities has suffered different problems with massive murders, and kidnapping due to a violent illegal drug trade. Italy with their present President Sergio Mattarella and Prime Minister Matteo Renzi has maintained old and new values of technology which is sometimes based on the activities in the Vatican City. Contrary to these facts both of these countries have existed without massive foreign terrorist attacks. This is the resource upon conflict of how some issues of death and violence is prevented or regulated with the viewing audience of television, the internet, and the maturity within peoples decision making. Otherwise these morals, ethics, and the overall level of national security becomes valuable for how to accept what content may be acceptable or unacceptable on the internet or television with logical and responsible use of commercial satellites.

Considering most well developed countries throughout the world they most all have satellite and radar systems as airplanes are capable of traveling to an airport runway landing with diversified conditions. Also cargo ships, and other sea vessels travel throughout the oceans of the world with a diversified array of products and even people that may require special accommodations. This becomes a theoretical concern between corporate businesses, and government. As these issues are considered along with communication systems, and even "human rights" issues, major concerns along with various good or bad conflicts within state owned small, large or corporate businesses are indifferent. Therefore occasionally some foreign government officials become closer to trying to own or dictate the people contrary to sadly dictating business.

As international business may occasionally consist of crime networks against American products and people, negligence or corrections by small and large American corporations become important. A vital observation that I have considered with Microsoft Corporation, Apple Computer

Incorporated, and a vast amount of other computer, satellite, and communication companies is that they call their data storage system the "cloud" which is discretionary. The cloud name is a nice, but somewhat an inaccurate term when its really a satellite system connected to their server systems for data memory. Considering the vast amount of inadmissible or invisible capabilities that satellites consist of the U.S. government needs a more solid format of affirmations. Theoretically this matter is conditional with the clouds in the sky not being "Man Made", but satellites, and computers with massive memory servers are "Controlled and Made by Man".

As Bill Gates, Paul Allen (Microsoft), Steve Jobs, Tim Cook (Apple), and a vast amount of other smart computer programmers, analysis, and businesspeople have excepted various terms like "the Cloud" this seems slightly misleading or indifferent. The conflicting understanding to a vast amount of Americans - is due to the use within understanding, and excepting the capabilities of satellites or how we have found technology to mislead an enormous amount of Americans, and especially children. Then from the plant Earth to Orbit and other planets this becomes a tremendous observation that is even shared throughout worldwide educational scholars whom seek these experimental values without harm to other humans.

Understanding these various issues Corporate America is very much so involved in technology issues along with the good, and bad of the American system of government. These factors of technology are part of how our American society has made advancements, but also must maintain the core values of human morality.

Human morality becomes the logic of how we as an international society of people reacts, and respects one another. This becomes the vital necessity of domestic tranquility that the United States Constitution outlines so that we can live peacefully together as people with logical values. These values are vital, but they have suffered tremendous levels of indifference. The indifference has been the reactions of coping with hearing voices, and people committing crimes with no logical motive, or just down right negligence that sometimes ends with industry or overall fatalities.

# METEOROLOGY, SCIENTIFIC PRINCIPALS, AND SATELLITES

(10)

## CHAPTER TEN

(10)

Anger and Technology In America

Worse Than The Watergate Crisis, Without Domestic Tranquility

# METEOROLOGY, SCIENTIFIC PRINCIPALS, AND SATELLITES

(10)

Satellites and the studies within meteorology that consist of scientific principals is part of man made products, or items, and nature that applies to weather and numerous social surroundings. Contrary to weather satellites on land, or in the outer space of orbit, this has given various professions, occupations, and government arbitrary resources of technology. Also this even applies to the United States Department of Defense with helpful disciplines of geological, and strategic war planning. Therefore as violent engagements of wars may consist of "dangerous and bad" weather there is a broad array of good, bad, and conflicting satellite use along with some internet activity that becomes important to observe.

Scientific principals in America is within the course of good, and bad methods or experiments that sometimes consist of valued levels of sociology. As of men and woman whom have died from dehydration (c/o Heat), or frostbit (c/o Cold), this means being prepared for dangerous or bad weather is vital. Hurricane Katrina, Ike, Sandy, and other storms lately have fallen into these categories of diversified weather, geology, and meteorology. Otherwise these are important and useful activities for weather satellites predicting snow, tornados, hurricanes, and other weather conditions from the National Oceanic and Atmospheric Administration (NOAA), and the National Weather Service providing critical forecast.

As meteorology, and sociology come together the concentration of improvements, or disasters become evident. This evidence has been displayed all over the United States since the 1960s, and then becoming severely complex or bad during the beginning of the early 1990s as an Endless Loop Crisis. These are sociological disasters with numerous people hearing voices that have destroyed families, schools systems, church establishments, and numerous other American values upon which attention was not applied to vital natural and scientific-principals. Gang violence with massive murders is truly one other factor, along with domestic murder, and occasional suicide. Some of these mass murders even includes children being killed which is another tremendous crisis with mostly unclear motives, therefore clear decisions about numerous issues has been vital.

Terrorism has become another strategic issue if you compare how on 9-11-2001 it was a nice September day in New York City until terrorist struck. This is similar to U.S. Department of Defense values of occasionally when to make a clear attack against an enemy nation. This has been an active issue of strategic planning during, and somewhat before World War II against France in the English Channel when the U.S. delayed their attack with allied forces for a "day" due to bad storms. These are also logical reasons why the U.S. government spends billions of dollars on research and development that applies to the U.S. Department of Defense (DOD), the National Weather Services, and other government operations.

Observing war strategies this was even the evidence with the Japanese attacking Pearl Harbor during the Franklin Roosevelt Presidential administration in 1941. That day in 1941 was the observation of making a clear attack on this Pearl Harbor -- Hawaii U.S. Naval base, -- intensifying the United States involvement in World War II. This seems to be the strategy that the 9-11 Report attackers used on that nice day on September 11, 2001 which took Americans by tragic surprise. Otherwise bad national security was displayed by the United States that led to 1 large building "the Pentagon" being damaged, 2 large buildings "the World Trade Centers" destroyed, 4 commercial airplanes crashed, and the killing of nearly 3,000 people being "mostly Americans".

It's logical to say that if our American system of government did not protect the Pentagon (DOD) on 9-11-2001 there is other vital issues and conflicts that were missed and not protected as well. Considering these facts the U.S. Attorney General's office was a revolving door starting with Janet Reno leaving in 2001 before 9-11, then Eric Holder (1 month acting), John Ascroft (4 years), and then Alberto Gonzales for a bit more than 2 years. Then from September 2007 to February 2009 there was 4 attorney generals Clement, Keisler, Mukasey, and Filip before Eric Holder's main tenure. Following the 2001 attacks America also observed massive issues of financial crimes by people from the United States, the Middle East, and other nations. These attorney general issues with stress also included hundreds of millions of dollars funded to Mexican illegal drug transactions.

Observing various issues in America were far from positive between 1991 to 2007 (especially thru Indiana & Illinois) some lawyers, judges, and a few others used satellites against innocent citizens and ignored ongoing National Security problems that were leading up to the 9-11

Report attacks. These professionals caused extreme problems without the best help from concerned Americans, as most logical American values suffered into numerous tragedies. Then as they felt good about ruining scientific-principals, good business relations, and domestic tranquility theoretically consisted of more National Security concerns which kept coming and getting worse.

As Americans suffered the enormous financial crisis that was observed during 2006, 2007, and 2008 this also effected millions of Americans in negative ways. This was a clear sign of how the American system of government fell weak to hurricane Katrina, the 9-11 Report attacks, a drug and gang war, and the financial crisis which became part of millions of American families being foreclosed on from their properties, and forced into bad or conflicting decisions.

Going back to the attacks on September 11, 2001 that were an issue of terrorism, and anger this was spreading throughout America, and various parts of the world as corrections were needed. Observing this issue I believe that various Americans have redirected Meteorology into "Spying on their Neighbors" as technological discrepancies. Then this only increased an illegal practice with foreign spices that wanted to do harm to Americans or control various businesses, industry, or the resources of money circulations (c/o paying taxes or not paying taxes) in America. Also this can be recognized, and or connected to the vast amount of Americans that are making efforts to leave the United States, and join groups like "Isis and or other Middle East terrorist organizations".

An "Endless Loop Crisis" conditionally describes a continuous circumference of tremendous illegal problems (c/o Satellites, or Computers with programs), and an amount of anger between various people, and some well developed countries. Also this even becomes a deterrent from the lawful Constitutional values that the American society was established by. The complexity of this is even more factually harmful to most young people, infant babies, and some older people. This is due to peoples lack of coping with lawful understandings of discipline, and people with health problems without good health solutions and conditioning.

Another "Endless Loop Crisis" has lately even included an outburst of police brutality issues which sometimes end up fatal. Contrary to this factor of brutality even police officers that are killed by criminals is part of a continuous angry society of people. These are people that have been misguided, or have not established any good direction in life besides a radical attitude, and various inappropriate ways of living.

Mainly, various issues of anger has become the difference between the authority, and anxiety of black, white, foreign nationalist, and other Americans (c/o police and government officials) with tremendous conflicting concerns, or high alert commands. Then contrary to satellite activity an array of people must be respectful or logical to the concentration of law enforcement, and citizen engagement. Police, government, the people, and various corporate American officials have diversified access to commercial satellites. Then a vast amount of times police understand their duties, and others may sway as they are not using these satellites to predict weather or communicate in lawful ways, but more so to obtain information lawfully and sometimes unlawfully which sometimes is an issue to instigate harm.

Contrary to government one corporate American conflict lately is the control of enormous amounts of money by "Hedge Fund" managers which is slightly similar to communism or dictators controlling discretionary wealth in undeveloped countries. These Hedge Funds also somewhat have put most logical mutual funds for small investors, and others out of business, even with their access to satellite technology. These are funds like Fidelity Investments Incorporated "Magellan Fund" formerly managed by Peter Lynch, which provided secured investments for most all investors involved. This consisted of a time during the 1970s, and 1980s that the American financial markets maintained more security, and lawful financial activity. Therefore as these investments compared to advancements in meteorology, satellites, and other technology legislature became vital to lawfully correct any bad or Unconstitutionally considered new products or services.

Considering the difference between hedge funds, and mutual funds is the indifference that more wealthy people profit from hedge funds, with small investors mostly not included, and taking various losses. These issues consist of more financial conflicts, and closely considered crimes which have become similar to Anti-Trust laws that apply to the control of hedge funds or monopolies. Therefore scientific principals with any "bad" human decision making becomes financially complex, harmful or may consist of harm that is instigated with other people making unlawful attacks with commercial satellites, and lately this consist of drowns being used in an unlawful capacity.

As satellite technology applies to a vast amount of U.S. Department of Defense officials with some civilians, certain satellites used unlawfully can be a U.S. Court Martial Offence established by presidential executive orders. These become the harmful neighborly spy's whom have more than likely created a tremendous amount of conflicts. Then tremendous conflicts such as these overstep a vast amount of human scientific-principals, and U.S. Constitutional laws. Considering these factors of "human and man made products" with the interventions of nature, or living naturally becomes confusing with a bewilderment to people making more so bad decisions. These are decisions that are being carried out as part of innocent people hearing voices penetrated mentally and instigated by an Endless Loop Crisis of uncontrollable, and or destructive issues of manipulation.

Understanding advancements in technology over the last two decades has also consisted of tremendous acts of violence that the majority of Americans observe as senseless. This part of anger and technology in America has then become two conflicts of social destruction, and the need of legislature that restricts bad technology, and satellite un-affirmed activities. These are issues that provoke violence or offer issues of criminal intent, and fatal or nonfatal negligence. Considering these factual issues, the American system of government "can not" achieve domestic tranquility without formal discussions, and detailed legislature concerning these matters. Contrary to these facts America is still making advancements in predicting weather with communications of radio, and television apart from any attempted crimes, and negligence with satellites, and this overrides some of the senseless conflicts of technology.

The intent of financial crimes, violent crimes, or negligence have become the negative results of cities like Detroit, Mi., Harrisburg, Pa., and a few others trying to overcome bankruptcy and other conflicts. People seriously making bad decisions is sometimes due to manipulation within a person's thinking as scientific-principals and or social standards consist of a low rate of ethics and efficiency. This becomes the loss of sovereignty that some Americans can't always control their destiny of domestic tranquility, and or prosperity without good, or the best decision making possible. Otherwise whether its financial crimes, violence, instigated crimes, negligence or other issues which may include fatalities the laws, and the Constitution must maintain its discipline or have balance. This is vital for the American people to survive with sovereignty that is prosperous.

When the term satellite office, or a satellite country as of a worldwide region being controlled by this technology with "ineffective activities, or disastrous issues" more than likely this can possibly make society worse or slightly insecure. These (c/o good and bad) commercial technology occurrences and activities in various regions of satellite control within anybody's life existence has some caution. Then there is usually discretionary values of domestic tranquility, and prosperity. Usually this is when all commercial and residential facilities consist of satellite dishes on the top of most residential and commercial buildings. As this is valuable to industry and some concerns of society a level of cautious awareness for natural living is valuable similar to reviews by the Federal Communication Commission or the National Weather Services.

These satellite regions and cities consist of various conditions of a lack of full sovereignty when the people are controlled by opinions of manipulated indifference apart from secured wired communication systems. Considering all information is not false, misleading, or manipulative the legal disciplines of Free Speech and Confidentiality under the 1$^{st}$ and the 4$^{th}$ Amendments has its pros and cons. This becomes the logic of AT&T along with other phone companies, television, and regional communication companies which government requires land lines, and wall plugs to be installed in most all newly constructed buildings as these systems have legal responsibilities.

Considering a value of wealth and opportunities are threatened along with the usefulness of meteorology, scientific-principals, various satellite activity, and even economic stability this can become efficient when lawful values are Constitutionally maintained. This is also similar to Americans having been frustrated when their jobs have been relocated to other states or countries. Just as this includes local American schools being closed, forcing the youth to travel across town day after day to be educated with academics, and scholastic resources making these adjustments complex.

As certain establishments such as remote villages or communities are in transition of unmanageable concerns, this occasionally can be observed within satellites causing a loss or lack of full sovereignty. These sovereignty issues are the lack of resources within valued scientific-principals that are vaguely or conditionally recognized for the vital survival of people, the environment of growing crops, or even the economy with effective government. Contrary to these facts a level of sovereignty is still important to observe with a vast amount of human values that keep society prosperous and normal. These become societies throughout the world that are working to become well developed or redeveloped regional establishments if no natural disasters, or constantly destructive terrorism or bad conflicts occur.

Upon comparison of new or old cities and or towns the concept of a well-developed society is based occasionally on progressive (c/o liberalism) values. These are progressive liberal (c/o conservatism) values that are important for the prosperity of the people, industry, government, and other resources. As the progressive sovereignty of redevelopment, restructuring, or a growing society of well-considered advancements are maintained a variation of opportunities, and tranquility becomes a priority. Therefore man made and womanly values are considered and used properly, along with other nature and societal issues such as diversified weather predictions. Then these factors most times must be managed with concern at a good regional capacity.

Tornados in America provide little understanding before striking. Then as they provide little time within bad weather predictions, this is an enormous issue of concern throughout various regions which are usually effected. Missouri, Oklahoma, Texas, Kansas, Arkansas, and other states have suffered extensive losses to tornados for centuries. Over the decades people and property have been destroyed from these vicious storms through the central states of America as cities and towns make strong efforts to recover. Understanding this tornados most times must be tracked or predicted from the lowest point and highest point with wind speed forces. This outlines the danger that the storm may consist of in reliable social livable standards.

The most complex scientific-principals that applies to tornados is how fast they develop, and the destructive damage, or deadly components of nature they produce. These are weather issues of meteorology that a vast amount of American cities depend on before they have been severely damaged by a tornado, and the complex understanding of their direction. Advanced satellite technology has lately given meteorologist a determination of the tracking and warning of these weather conditions of nature that are considerably harmful. Observing these matters of diversion some property, and human protection can be effective.

Another fact within moving or advancing conditions of technology in America is increasing the speed within lawful and unlawful communication voice, and computer information transitions as the laws, and the Constitution becomes vital issues. Satellites and communication systems have outlined this factor within the vast amount of Americans that hear voices in the commercial airspace which is a scientific-principal that needs to be corrected, and or maintained lawfully. Therefore as these levels of scientific-principals violates the U.S. Constitution and other laws the American people and society is occasionally being severely victimized.

NASA, NOAA, NSA, and others have access to these technological systems similar to major corporations and or professional computer programming analyst that manufacture and whom programs satellites, computers, and other levels of technological equipment. Even American television stations, and "foreign television stations" operating in America along with various internet businesses consist of high speed information technology. A certain level of appropriate viewing audiences have discovered this to be good, and sometimes occasionally horrifying. Then for massive amounts of people it becomes hopeful that good decision making is applied against any level of indecency, or destructive acts that may include being an enemy to the United States.

Observing the United States Department of Homeland Security which was established a few years after the 2001 terrorist attacks, before this an enormous amount of complex violations of law occurred. These law violations consisted of Illegal and Hazardous Commercial Satellite use which has done severe damage to hundreds of thousands of American people. The damage was complex mostly violating these peoples 1$^{st}$ and 4$^{th}$ Amendment Constitutional rights.

So leading up to the September 11, 2001 terrorist attacks people of an international and U.S. domestic condition of radical views, and nationalism have caused great harm, and destruction with their access to commercial satellites and other technology. Then due to the people that are mostly Americans like Andrea Yates, Aaron Alexis, Adam Lanza (Sandy Hook), Eric Harris, Dylon Klebold (Columbine), Steven Kazmierczak (Northern Illinois Univ.), and thousands of other Americans with lower of similar complex violent crimes, they seem to be victims that were coerced into some of our nations worse domestic crimes. Therefore the scientific-principals of the American society along with legislature and enforcing these resources of law that may surround good, and more so bad meteorology and satellites use - have critical domestic tranquility work during these 1$^{st}$ few decades of the 2000 millennium.

# PSYCHOLOGY, MEDICINE, AND AMERICAN SATELLITE TECHNOLOGY

(11)

# CHAPTER ELEVEN

(11)

Anger and Technology In America

Worse Than The Watergate Crisis, Without Domestic Tranquility

# PSYCHOLOGY, MEDICINE, AND AMERICAN SATELLITE TECHNOLOGY

(11)

The determination between psychology, medicine, and American satellite activity holds numerous values of concern that should not destroy the American people, and the society we live in. This psychology (c/o psychiatry) within anger and technology in the United States goes along the line of issues such as all medicine, satellites, and a vast amount of large ticket items are not all ways perfectly normal for everyone. A powerful example is how the Food and Drug Administration approved the medication Zoloft made by the Pfizer Company. Considering this Anti-Depressant (Zoloft) numerous people became worse off (c/o sickness & side-effects) with a number of people whom died from its use. Therefore it was reviewed through the U.S. federal government and the courts with certain law suits filed, and argued that medical problems were not corrected.

Considering product liability concerns goes along the issued subjects of Artificial Intelligence, this is based on cyber/spectrum networks similar to computer operating systems that operate lawfully, secure, and safe. Occasionally these become products that are not always prefect before extensive product recalls, evaluations, and or revisions. Therefore people may suffer on occasions from these advanced products or the services that they offer which are a provision by other physicians, pharmaceutical corporations, and or various business concerns.

Observing the fact that satellite product and design revisions upon business and government oversight are vital to correct, this becomes critical with the more products, and technology we have available. The correction and advancements of various products is a valuable concern as it sometimes requires more logical regulation which becomes important, and vital. This means there are some products, and even more so some non-subscribed or unwanted satellite activities along with services that prove to be illegal and cautiously destructive to the American general public. Similar to public, private, corporate businesses, and government certain negligence becomes time consuming argumentative problems with damage just like the BP (Amoco Corp) Texas City, Texas oil refinery explosion in 2005. This accident took years to settle, evaluate, and regroup from before another BP explosion in the Gulf of Mexico during 2010.

Other products contrary to those of "Pharmaceutical Companies" with internal medicine products that are in logical demand by patients, but occasionally observed with prescribed caution are a vital part of American professionalism. These are products that become needed, but occasionally unwanted (c/o product satisfaction and dependability) within logical nature. Then there are other products that are less complex, and more common than psychology, medicine, lasers, and satellites. Those products are automobiles that have been recalled with defects lately at record numbers.

Considering all automakers throughout the United States in 2004 a fraction of more than 30 million automobiles were recalled, and in 2014 some 60 million were recalled. This process was sped up due to the causes of an increase within deaths, and injuries. A comparison of satellites that don't have many recalls compared to automobiles have been intervening with technological issues of artificial intelligence. These factors include numerous satellite components that can control vital automobile parts, sensors, and even remotely drive the vehicle. In 2015 it was determined that general intelligence or "common sense or ground values" had a need to be corrected with a few of Chrysler (c/o Fiat) vehicle models which can be operated by computer hackers. Therefore this recall effected 1.4 to 11 million hack-able "Fiat-Chrysler" vehicles with the U.S. Department of Transportation considering fines of $105 million dollars.

General Motors (GM), and Honda have contributed to a vast amount of these recalls during the first 2 decades of the 2000s. This was observed with GM ignition switches failing, and other recall details causing death, and injuries which cost GM Corp more than $2.7 billion in 2014 with some fines from government. Honda's airbags (by Takata Corp) have been dangerously inflating with metal particles busting the bag, and exploding in the faces of the vehicle's operators, and passengers. Considering there has been these and other products that look good, but had defective parts these discretionary products have been proven dangerous along with their effort of technological advanced disciplines of operating capacity.

Companies like General Electric, Boeing, Raytheon, American Telephone &Telegraph (AT&T), and Microsoft along with the government's National Aeronautics and Space Administration (NASA), the National Oceanic and Atmospheric Administration (NOAA), and Landsat are major satellite business partners. This group within business and government are also part of the developers team of commercial satellites which includes some system programming, and manufacturing. Therefore they also do research and development similar to automobile companies, but recalls or revisions are slightly more complex. This is due to expert or complex programmers, and operators of these highly technical large ticket items, and their operating systems.

The determination of psychology and safe satellite use is most times affirmed to the people without the general public being misinformed, diagnosed with prognostications, or them being drastically confused about various subjects. Then this form of psychology (c/o psychiatry), internal medicine, and commercial or residential satellite use can be determined safe or unsafe with most times unlawful inadmissible directions or affirmations. These are products and services that have occasionally caused anger, sickness, certain illnesses, financial distress leading to economic disasters, and or even death.

Internal medicine in America is a valued and astute concept of business and scientific levels of medical resources. Contrary to the importance of internal medicine along with psychology, psychiatry, and certain active commercial satellites there have been people effected with increasing mental health challenges. Sometimes this is observed as a doctors diagnoses of the persons metal challenges which may have been a prognostication of symptoms which have been a critical problem, and mistake. Then to have a full psychological or psychiatric recovery including with certain prescribed medicines being the best or logical solution this requires more time, money, and evaluated decisions.

An important observation in the courts is between the expert testimonies within Doctors of Internal Medicine VS the Engineering, Astrology, Meteorology, and or Geology professional expert testimonies VS the Defendant and complex violators. This might include government constituents and certain disastrous issues that must be corrected. Observing astrologist, geologist, meteorologist, and some engineers occasionally their testimony is due to their access to powerful satellite equipment that may commonly be used. Contrary to "Top Secret U.S. government projects" a vast amount of satellite activity that is inadmissible or with non-affirmed acknowledgment from satellite operations, various negative activities may occur. This becomes extensive along with broad subjects within some good issues, and more un- affirmed problems. These problems are consistent and constant by various questionable people violating various laws with extremely dangerous opinions making issues complex for the courts decisions to have the right expert witnesses with testimony evidence.

As these become complex arguments for the courts that thrive on admissible evidence, various other mistakes, prognostications, and misguided decisions with bad opinions occurred without people being part of the best solutions. So in some cases the courts, lawyers, and doctors (c/o other professionals within expert witnesses) missed certain important "scientific principals" (c/o wireless satellite systems) that a vast amount of normal people may, or have suffered from. Therefore this then is not to say all people are influenced by satellite activity, but with artificial intelligence certain major problems likely will or may occur. Also this has caused circumstances that if they are not corrected, some people becoming worse in America is part of an Endless Loop Crisis concern that needs to be evaluated before violence or disaster is a complex factor.

Anger within people whom are not always radically mad, and whom have end up committing domestic murder, or mass murders with occasional suicide whom did not always fully recover with psychotropic medications, and or treatments are a concern of various issues. Basically the victim whom became a defendant (c/o an Endless Loop Crisis) in the courts, may have stop taking a medicine that more than likely was a bad experience or with bad side-effect reactions, contrary to medicine that helps. This very well may be where conflicts of a prognostication have been part or some causes within a motive to become more angry than normal, or with anger that continues to build up over time occasionally turning into extensive violence.

Considering the numerous diagnosed illnesses that are caused by man made products, chemicals, or dangerous plants, animals, and or even the environment have effected various people, and some industries. This becomes the logic of government having duties to correct these public health issues or hazardous concerns, but sometimes government involvement is way to late within helping certain people. Then other issues, and people whom have caused illness, injuries, conflicts, and or even mysterious fatalities with unlawful satellites, or lasers must be observed as a legal problem. Therefore they must be taken under the lawful enforcement of government (c/o the courts) to keep these technological industry standards, and activities Constitutionally lawful, and safe.

The Constitutions of various state governments, and the United States government is livable, but in need of vital amendments as technology advances in good, and sometimes with bad details that must be corrected.

This becomes the logic that the more advanced American technology and business establishments American people have available, the more we must take note and make corrections when it becomes a severe level of harm to a massive amount of people. Then this has been recognized 1000s of times with less complex technology than satellites, but this means that the American system of government must change with these times of advanced issues of technology. Therefore this vitally includes how the courts review various issues, and diversified technology law cases.

Basically the more people whom don't understand how to get various legal matters through the courts, the more prosecutors, judges, government or corporate officials, and some other community members may misunderstand, ignore, or insult people as victims with them becoming defendants. This becomes a vital concern over the true integrity of these highly advanced violations of law. Otherwise these violations of law are complex and inadmissible to innocent people contrary to major crime organizations that some officials want to occasionally associate innocent people with concerning their conflicting level of involvement.

Numerous business or corporate products in America has had to go through some process of revisions ether through the government recommendations or responsible business decisions. This applies to various products offered to the American general public, but this is usually for the good of all progress unless certain individual citizens or the state and federal government outlines steps to take to correct any problems properly. As numerous other professionals especially in the medical industry recognize this extensive issue as an increase in violence occurs without a logical motive, the courts, lawyers, and logical experts have a logical reason to argue. Then they seem to be occasionally counted within some people as government officials that don't care to argue these vital issues of scientific-principals that include sometimes financial matters of damage.

On occasions Northwest Indiana and a vast amount of other places like in Evansville, Indiana with a high rate of suicide between 2007 and 2009 took observation of social issues, and not scientific principal conflicts. This was relevant by the partial solution of Vanderburgh (Indiana) County Coroner - Don Erk, but only minor issues seem to improve. Considering the first decade of 2000, which became disastrous to Indiana and a vast amount of other states, these issues have seem to have support or be slightly be considered incompetent with statements of somebody being just crazy or on drugs. Then it becomes somewhat complex too clam that this is only about destructive satellite activity (c/o bad judges and other officials) as there was a need for constructive law arguments.

As some people throughout America have even instigated certain levels of harm which forced a vast amount of young and a few older people to commit mass murder, murder, and or occasional suicide a solution to this anger did not seem to go away. This neurological issue of scientific principals between satellites and how peoples "brains or thought processes" are effected is different from the frequencies of "TV, car or radio antennas". Then this has shifted the logic of needing medicine, to our American society or needing satellite regulation enforcement.

Entrapment laws by a judge or court officials which may include the use of commercial satellites is something that 10s of thousands of innocent Americans can not afford, or have trouble with the knowledge or convenient authority to argue in a court of law. With any other infractions of law violations the American system of government in Indiana has given some judges like Karen F. Wilson of Gary, Indiana and a few others including William Daly of Chicago the authority of pervasive dictators. As William Daly worked for Ameritech Corp he had conflicting access to commercial satellites which he pursued extremely unlawful and illegal use. This even applies to complacent government officials that instigated conflicts against people with strong professional values, and they were replaced by various unproductive people including others like illegal aliens from Mexico that don't speak or understand the English language.

I strongly considered these issues mysterious during an Endless Loop crisis in which a plane crash killed Commerce Security Ron Brown (with others and some staff members), then soon after another plain crash killed Congressman Mickey Leland of Texas, and a local Gary Judge - James Kimbrough died in a strange car accident. Following that, numerous manufacturing facilities consisted of fatal explosions, and other engineering, and technical construction accidents along with massive infant mortality. This means the people of Gary, and throughout the United States have loss some values of attention span, and slightly unarguably domestic tranquility. Also this goes along the lines within critical decisions, and how the Separation of Powers has not held logical balance. As it applies to a humans attention span Illegal and Hazardous Commercial Satellite use is causing various extensive non-tranquility voice transmissions which can totally disrupt someone's attention span at sometimes the most critical times.

The discrepancy within the Separation of Powers occasionally makes the judicial branch (c/o the local or lower courts) and jail more powerful when operating from "artificial intelligence" and not "general intelligence". Conditionally any other branches (c/o high or low levels) of government then do not have the theory that - No One Branch Of American Government Is More Powerful Than The Other. I presume this is why some people whom are incarcerated within the Department of Correction in America have been pardoned by U.S. Presidents like Bill Clinton, George Bush, and Barack Obama during their last years in office. This makes the Separation of Powers an equation of logical "value or resource of existence".

Observing various issues of angry people in America that don't have the psychological disciplines and tolerance to endure being a victim of Illegal and Hazardous Commercial Satellite use, they usually brake down in negative and complex ways. Understanding this, internal medicine rarely helps completely, and observing some people in the American society of government committing these crimes, other people as victims with complex inadmissibility conflicts have very little help or support if any. Then even the U.S. National Security Administration (NSA) becomes somewhat unhelpful in various ways by not enforcing complex international and domestic laws. Also this vitally includes our values of tranquility which is causing harm to productive Americans leaving foreign people with a sense of control. Therefore when using this technology to manipulate American small business owners, this has given the American society levels of weakness and vulnerability. Then this has appropriated numerous ways for foreign people to have access within gaining control of vital small, large, and some corporate businesses including vital industry concerns in America.

These factors of good, and bad foreign relation issues is part of the psychology within American peoples decision making values to observe, and plan for the future hopefully without anger. Even as America has loss control of a vast amount of businesses to foreign owners, the control or containment of anger is diversified within people. Understanding this, is like considering how peaceful, and economically secure life could be in coming years even as it applies to the advancements of commercial satellites. Also this vitally includes wireless communications, but Americans hopefully must hold strong and wise to the laws, and or legislature because of the complex issues that this technology consist of psychologically. Then truly observing some issues of advanced technology for peace, and domestic tranquility have seem to be nearing last place within numerous large or small populated cities, and towns that suffered in diversified ways.

One issue about the majority of American citizens of a populated region apart from some large cities is the anger of U.S. citizens that are placed in last place due to a lack of prosperity, and opportunity. With commercial satellites, other technology, and economic opportunities is working more for foreign immigrants apart from the thought process of most American born people being isolated. Their isolated conflicts have consisted of the psychology that certain people are becoming extremely wealthy through the financial markets, contrary to the extent of them working secure jobs. Then a massive amount of Americans that are vaguely having financial opportunities to survive become frustrated with isolation, vulnerability, and sometimes hopelessness.

The United States has not always been prefect, but the logic of perfection is considered in many ways. From the NASA space program, the agriculture industry, internal medicine, major engineering and construction projects, and other industries which may consist of fabricating satellites have helped in various detailed and positive ways. Contrary to this fact various developing countries working through the United Nations becomes an international concern for laws that appropriate these resourceful values within diversified treaties. The treaties apply to policies organized by: the Committee on the Peaceful Uses of Outer Space, and the secretariat Office of Outer Space Affairs. Also this includes the Conference on Disarmament that negotiates arms control, and disarmament that conditionally prevents an arms race in outer space. Therefore America and a vast amount of the World's most powerful nations with advanced technology do try to work together for progress, and hopeful peace with prosperity.

# ARTIFICIAL INTELLIGENCE, U.S. INDUSTRY, & GENERAL INTELLIGENCE

(12)

# CHAPTER TWELVE

(12)

Anger and Technology In America

Worse Than The Watergate Crisis, Without Domestic Tranquility

# ARTIFICIAL INTELLIGENCE, U.S. INDUSTRY, & GENERAL INTELLIGENCE

(12)

The alliance of artificial intelligence (c/o computers, robots, and satellites verses and compared to humans) along with various industries in the United States works to create and establish a sense of logic and foundation within general intelligence. This transition of products, and services (c/o industry), or even research that applies to lawful and safe technology operating or usage standards for the "General Public" becomes a vital part, and level of American efficiency and legally "affirmed responsibilities". Then these are standards that are to be consistent, and applicable to most individual state Constitution's, and the Constitution of the United States without producing anger or destruction, and therefore maintaining domestic tranquility.

Contrary to various intelligent technology within products and services, America has numerous activities and issues of liability within technological concerns which must be reviewed by law, and or legislature. This consist of the good, and bad legal format of some people in public, private businesses whom should have strong levels of liability along with government. These are people whom use "satellite technology" (c/o good and bad liabilities) with television, radio, and diversified telephone companies, but not ruling out the U.S. Central Intelligence Agency (CIA) or the National Security Agency (NSA)" observing a level of strategic intelligence.

The United States Central Intelligence Agency along with artificial intelligence becomes a vital issue (c/o international conflicts) of how this technology was not used to prevent the attacks on September 11, 2001. This was a terrorist act harming the people in the New York World Trade Center towers, the Pentagon, and the destruction of 4 major commercial airplanes killing altogether around 3,000 people. Otherwise government and the elite amount of others did not save American assets, and various peoples lives during the 9-11 terrorist attacks that should have been prevented.

Understanding satellites within good and more so bad people, and some corporate American activity including government with various responsibilities to protect the American people and society as it applies to lawful disciplines of technology has occasionally been misguided. This has consisted of instigated business anticompetitive practices, and antisocial conflicts with mistakes, infractions of law, and some court martial offenses. Then this becomes a diversified issue whether being a law binding concern, and or valued commitment for safe and responsible "satellite or other technology" usage. The concept of regulated usage was observed between 1958 and 1962 after the Congress established a civilian space agency in the National Aeronautics and Space Act of 1958.

During the 1962 John F. Kennedy Presidential Administration the Communications Satellite Act of 1962 was passed by Congress. This effected a limited amount of companies (+/-10) like American Telephone & Telegraph (AT&T) due to their use and control of wired communications, and more so their worldwide communication operating disciplines. Other communication companies had opposition because of AT&T's majority worldwide market control including some U.S. Department of Defense contract resources. As other companies had some opposition to this legislature the concentration of decisions and compromise came from an AT&T proposed joint ownership of all communications satellites. This was to make satellites more attainable with private communication companies having access for their customers and business operation.

The joint ownership decision by AT&T to work together with other communication companies without anticompetitive discrepancies, or antitrust law violations was a valued understanding, contrary to the understanding of any effects to the people which occasionally becomes an important concern. Observing effects to the people as communication or non-communication customers is a valid concern that lately has created and instigated some issues of anger, and confusion. The format of this is the consideration that America concentrated on the utilization power of satellites, but not the domestic tranquility that some satellite activity can instigate or produce. Therefore as a public utility the business and social control of a market of people must be considered Constitutionally safe from a lawful monopolizing process, and not unlawful harmed.

Other technological corporate American industry concerns are American Broadcasting Company (ABC), National Broadcasting Company (NBC), Columbia Broadcasting System Crop. (CBS), and various others including cable networks which have expanded along with television and radio satellite resource with occasional discipline. This is factual along with foreign networks including British Broadcasting Corporation (BBC), and the Al Jazeera television network whom even have a determination to spy and use information to harm Americans and other nationalities in numerous ways. Then this also includes the effect on small and large business activities of value with some foreign conflicting control that has been established by satellite transmissions. Therefore with good, bad, lawful, and or unlawful issues of active technology which satellites are used by people, will find ways to get into trouble, cause harm, or even make good prosperous decisions with newly advanced products.

As it applies to the well-being of people living in a technological environment within a lawful and prosperous society, regulation has needs that are to be just as advanced as useable technology. Then this means working to maintain domestic tranquility which has been lacking during the 1990s, and 2000s which some people have continuously "done and got" it wrong. Then this becomes the issue of unlawful use and will they get into trouble and be prosecuted to end a bad crisis.

A logical definition of "Artificial Intelligence" is the intelligence exhibited by machines, robots, computers, computer software, satellite systems, and a few other complex products. This intelligent behavior becomes effective for thousands or more products and services applicable to cell phones, television networks, radio stations, and now conditionally satellite imagery, contrary to most agriculture or live-stock natural products or various commodities. Then this becomes effective to millions of people that sometimes don't understand these "Earth to Orbit" products and operating systems of advanced technology.

As cable television has expanded with even foreign owners, Americans have seem to except numerous diversified programs, but a level of suffering has also occurred. Suffering in America can be observed in at least two (2) ways which is for one; people don' receive T.V. and Radio Signals in a lawful or affordable way, and 2$^{nd}$; with Satellite T.V. and Radio more foreign people and Americans acting unlawful with this complex technology is causing innocent people to be victimized until they become defendants of crimes. Then from people hearing voices with no identifiable affirmation which disturbs their conscious level of awareness, and decisions making "disaster is almost inevitable".

Contrary to the vital consciousness of innocent people, then as satellite television and radio has transitioned our American society with more technology the Federal Communication Commission (FCC) has not considered if artificial intelligence from the airways is causing people more harm than good. This harm is associated with people hearing voices, and then conditionally almost forced or provoked those victimized people to act within non-humanity values in a course of anger, and or violence. In the future it is vital that the FCC, various state agencies, and others in government correct this issue of an endless loop crisis.

The most observed study contrary to making American people angry with artificial intelligence consist of academic studies upon which certain activities become a logical sense of "General Public Intelligence" apart from artificial intelligence that has not become a full concept of general intelligence. This becomes important within how the American society establishes "industry standards" that are part of government regulation, even as it applies to a computer program acting in an Endless Loop mode. Then these ongoing regulated subjects of creating computers, computer software, and even sensors that are used with hundreds of products including satellites can provide safe, efficient, and lawful activities including (4th Amendment) affirmations.

Understanding more so advanced products which are considered astute (c/o good and bad values) within old expanding technology, and new technology standards the general public and government must work together to root out bad corporate or individuals satellite activity. These are mostly conditions of regulated satellite usage that small and large companies, corporations, and others are to lawfully abide by in their continuous level of business services or production. To observe how the Constitution's 4th Amendment is effected "The Words"; "to be secure in their persons, houses, papers, and effects, against unreasonable searches"; comes into action or with activities of communication satellites, geo-synchronous satellites creating computer satellite imagery, and other satellite sensors which can track objects, and people in their cars or houses becoming a conflicting problem. Considering these facts very few law enforcement officials or white collar criminals don't easily provide logical affirmations just like the "bad" of some prosecutors, various professionals, the CIA, the NSA, and a few others.

Observing CIA, NSA, and other government officials who pursue destructive illegal unofficial activities, inappropriate conduct, or whom have dangerous games to play with unlawful conspiracies against people who are not trying to commit a destructive crime, "synthetic consciousness" seems to occur. The amount of people suffering from synthetic consciousness has become a major objective with so much violence it sometimes consist of no logical or relevant motive. This seem to happen with Kevin Isom, Andrea Yates, Steven Kazmierczak, and others that killed people and or themselves. Some of these people seem to be sleepwalking while looking conscious, but feeling that they were slightly unconscious.

My opinion is that Seung-Hui-Cho on the campus of Virginia Tech was acting as a kamikaze extremist which is just as bad as observing one of the worse mass murders and suicide issue on a college campus in American history. Some of this violence comes from instigated conflicts or opinions of a vast amount of other people (c/o diversified violence) that are - or were never prosecuted. Then they continue to destroy people's lives with their anonymous satellite activity which occasionally causes unconscious-able thinking. This is because these issues supposedly are too complex for the courts to here until certain people are sometimes dead, socially mixed up, or financially destroyed.

As anger and violence has increased in the United States - so has artificial intelligence which means some technology is not regulated effectively or efficiently, and or certain complex laws are not enforced through government. This becomes the extensive economic and social problem when criminals or sometimes "So-Called" good people including some people in government learn new technological ways to violate the rights of citizens or even potential business owners as an anti-competitive or anti-social practice. Also this becomes the conspired Anti-Trust, Anti-Terrorist, and occasionally Anti-Gang legal concern that most local and individual state governments don't argue along with various agencies or the U.S. federal government fast enough to save people from "victim-hood" going into "defendant-hood".

Opinionated conflicts in the commercial airspace by bad collage sorority, and fraternity members and or Anti-Human, homosexual, transsexual activist who cause social and economic conflicts that push American prosperity backwards are part of personal value deprecation. This has caused some American businesses to suffer especially in black communities including men and woman relationships and or marriage to suffer along with even the loss of potential economic prosperity instigating "losses for other Americans". These are losses due to the insecurity of a mix between various small businesses and government which is an occupational, professional and government relationship to prosper with domestic tranquility. Otherwise this then includes Tax Revenue losses, and losses to our Constitutional law level of security.

An unpredictable logic which becomes non-prosperous for the entire American society effecting most locally governed citizens has caused awareness of various issues of anger. Within these compounds of economic hardships where people have to be mindful within making good decisions becomes complex with artificial intelligence. Then as artificial intelligence is not common sense (c/o man verse machinery) there are certain people who have tried to control other people's thoughts by using satellites anonymously which have occasionally succeeded with sometimes various destructive results. Artificial intelligence has consisted of studies where computers or other technology like robots are part of an effort to be equal to the human brain as this now becomes the issue with satellite technology. If this is used without lawfully affirmed research, the results on people unaware of it can be drastic like threatening the "existence of children and mankind".

In various parts of the United States the existence of mankind has continuously been threatened with mass murders, domestic murder including suicide, adults, and parents killing children including other violence. These crimes have very little motive or understanding especially when a vast amount of these people (c/o mental alterations) are killing children whom the defendant or killer has never knew. Then this is where the Computer and Satellite industries including the International Telecommunications Satellite Organization (INTELSAT) are on a path of occasionally causing human extinction. Observing these human and societal levels of self-destructing conditions some computer and satellite technology has over stepped "artificial and general artificial intelligence" as an "Artificial Intelligence Takeover".

A motive in the mist, of an "Artificial Intelligence Takeover" is conditionally like living in the most unpredictable world or an American society self-destructing before our historical eyes, and logical understanding. Then as most Americans can remember over the last 2 decades between 1995 and 2015 we have witnesses a vast amount of the worse disasters, and mass murders in the history of America. Apart from the indifference of workable artificial intelligence, certain disasters like September 11, 2001, hurricane Katrina (2005) along with the 2 BP incidents of the Gulf of Mexico explosion and oil spill (2010), and the BP (Amoco) Texas City, Texas oil Refinery explosion (2005) could have been prevented. Also people like U.S. Commerce Security Ron Brown, the discretionary loss of Michael Jackson (c/o sleep disorders) just like Elvis Presley, or Jimmy

Hendricks, and recently numerous mass murders has provided an objective that something is conditionally or occasionally wrong.

Paul Allen the co-founder of Microsoft Corp is critical with awareness that certain artificial intelligence is not likely to be excepted in this century. As this concept of logic within the good, and bad of satellites and robotic advancements in technology needs to vitally continue with overall public safety legislature, and U.S. Constitutional law disciplines as this more than likely will need to be observed with appropriate enforcement. Therefore even as computer and satellite programmers including analyst debug an endless loop artificial intelligence takeover from bad users of commercial satellites -- Americans are asking the question of why is so much violence, and anger being displayed with no motive in our well developed society.

Some studies have outlined that a robot or satellites in close comparison to the human brain, and including human activated resources can have the possibility to produce an artificial intelligence takeover. Contrary to an artificial intelligence takeover between violent video games, and an increasing amount of people suffering mental brake-downs, it seems that this is an argumentative takeover. This takeover within controlling factors have occurred with people using technology that can harm other humans as they sometimes may not know or care about dangerous or hazardous scientific-principals. These have become the broad satellite factors of metal, physical, financial, and even diversified fatal harm that lately has reached historical levels of tragedy.

As Americans have and can go to war in Iraq and Afghanistan for the violent terror on September 11, 2001 we conditionally have a domestic terror of similar concern. These levels of domestic terror at home have reached historical levels of disaster. Then government and a vast amount of citizens have not consisted of business, societal, and government solutions that have been applied to certain violent anger, or an appropriated fix to this American crisis.

In comparison the Iraq and Afghanistan war on a vast amount of occasions is a discretionary issue apart from certain neighborhoods in various American major cities. This is factual upon the cities whom have had more daily gang violence along with innocent citizen casualty murders than the casualties of American solder's on daily activities in our recent war's. This violent gang and social terror has occurred in Chicago, Philadelphia, Gary, Detroit, Los Angeles, New Orleans, Miami, and other metropolitan areas. Then contrary to major city streets, overall levels of terror consist of the violent activities at movie theaters, shopping malls, numerous schools, and other places that were considered to be safe at most times.

If an artificial intelligence takeover is evident and was to be prevented by the enforcement of laws, the U.S. government and various individual states have got it wrong, or they did not want it to be lawful. An example is that in a lengthy paper published by Linda L. Haller and Melvin Sakazaki (c/o the FCC) on "Commercial Space and United States National Security (2001)" it outlined the need or activity of advanced satellite activities. Contrary to workable products, this is similar to new products that sometimes don't work properly, or they cause fatal death or harm in certain ways which means these products must be recalled for revisions. Considering this paper which discussed a hopeful future, and present satellite activity in America we have not achieved all benefits discussed in that lengthy paper, report, and or document. Actually some of the large professional firms mentioned in the study like Bear Stearns Investments -- the 100+ year old brokerage firm went bankrupt, and fouled similar to others to never operate in business again.

A January 23, 1970 Executive Order of the President (Richard Nixon), "described" in the 2001 Commercial Space and National Security paper submitted a memorandum to the FCC (c/o Licensing Communication Systems) with at least 6 satellite policy objectives. Two of these objectives were; Minimizing regulator and administrative impediments to technological and market developments by the private sector. A second objective was; Discouraging anticompetitive practices that inhibit growth of healthy communications, and related services. Now contrary to other objectives like Emergency Preparedness, Public Economic Service Potential, and a few others -- Americans have been hit in various negative ways that comparably go far back into other disastrous historical acts, and problems.

Anticompetitive practices and administrative impediments go along the lines of issues that may be worse than the Watergate scandal and crisis. Then as there has been disputes between Americans in business and government foreign people have gained control of various vital small, and large corporate businesses including with terrorism and or anticompetitive issues of conflict. So historical acts and problems have become worse on American soil in diversified ways. These disasters of comparison are similar to the Great Depression (1929), the Pearl Harbor attacks (1942), contrary to the mage bankruptcies of the 80s, 90s, and the economic crisis surrounding 2007 which includes various times and acts of civil unrest with riots.

Considering the United States various Executive Orders have been established with not enough enforcement, and serious values of discipline. This is the logic that when an executive order is created and signed by the President of the United States various departments, agencies, and commissions need to forcefully apply a resourceful format within duties. Then this is observed within the case and issued concerns of the "Manual for Court-Martial United States (MCM), and especially its Article 106. Observing lawful discipline of court martial offences by military and or civilians some wording has changed after I made years of complaints about this sophisticated level of spying. Then even domestically against American neighbors or local businesses the wording changed and various acts of violence got worse with other conflicts having unclear motives.

Another study outlines that an Artificial Intelligence Takeover consist of the idea and logical concern that this kind of takeover may or would have the capability of recursive self-improvement "in robots", and more so in the natural brain of humans. This has occurred in what some people and professionals consider as an intelligent explosion which is part of what is observed as super-intelligence. So as computers, robots, and satellites can be actively superior to humans, this would make life difficult for humans to predict what it could do, making it almost or sometimes entirely unpredictable. We as Americans have witnessed this level of unpredictable violence, fatal manufacturing and refinery explosions, massive levee brake's with flooding, and other concerns observing over 20 years of tragedies in a comparison of time more than the past 100 years in American history.

# HISTORICAL DISASTERS, TRAGEDIES, TOLERANCE AND LIBERTY
(13)

## CHAPTER THIRTEEN
(13)

Anger and Technology In America

Worse Than The Watergate Crisis, Without Domestic Tranquility

# HISTORICAL DISASTERS, TRAGEDIES, TOLERANCE AND LIBERTY

(13)

The understanding of historical disasters in America along with human tolerance, and the liberty to control and or instigate anger has been part of the evaluation, and lawful needed improvements of domestic tranquility. This has lately been a critical value of concern, both with or without artificial intelligence technology. Also this includes unlawful activities by various people and technology use that occasionally do not care or recognize the domestic tranquility format of liberty, and various Constitutional laws. Even as hurricanes and tornados have given Americans tremendous damage we can't stop, or control easily - other disasters, and tragedies that must be observed for preventative measures or correction. Observing this during the years of 1990 to 2015 have consisted of some of America's most historical levels of diversified disasters, and tragic acts of violence without any logic of certain repulsive acts madness.

Contrary to violent gang activities and crime certain acts like the Oklahoma City bombing (1995), the 9-11 Report Terrorist attacks, mass murders like the Sandy Hook Elementary school shooting massacre, the Columbine High shooting, the Virginia Tech shooting (2007) massacre, the Boston Marathon bombing, and numerous acts of domestic murder and unlawful conditions. These acts have transpired more disasters, and tragedies then normal times in America. Also these are the crisis concerns that most logically good Americans don't want to tolerate. The most extreme level of artificial intelligence with or without direct human intervention (c/o satellites or computers) have not helped solve or stabilize these crisis concerns. Therefore the excessive amount of people committing these violent acts, and the families of the deceased victims are somewhat in the darkness of bewilderment about why these tragedies have happened so rapidly which seems to be through shear instigation.

Understanding the tolerance of a vast amount of Americans, this overall crisis within problems have endured the test of time, and has overwhelmingly included the tested values of technological artificial intelligence. This observation includes the somewhat inadmissibility of good, and bad commercial satellite use, and advanced computer science disciplines of complex products and services which has created a broad reality of American involvement. As government and a vast amount of professionals don't recognize or care to correct this disastrous crisis, more tragedies are more than likely to occur. Then the American system of government "must" apply improved regulative duties to protect the domestic tranquility of an overwhelming amount of American citizens.

Along with an enormous level of indifferent, good, and more so destructively bad decision making means America is moving backwards with children, and young adults being fatally shot, and horrified with untrustworthy social values. This has occurred in elementary schools, all the way up to collages, universities, and other public/private establishments. These institutions pay governed tax dollars or provide publicly supported values of faithful resources for high standards of safety and morals. Then also this has included other establishments that normally were considered safer than facilities where people usually are becoming a victim of violent and deadly activities. Otherwise various people seem to be a target not just by terrorist, but their own fellow misguided Americans.

As Americans have established, and understand some factors of liberty and decision making, the concentration of that liberation of values has had to become part of discipline, and logically controlled responsibilities. A brief and logical definition of Liberty - is the condition of being free from unlawful restriction "or" control, but lately more money has been spent on security measures that vaguely reduce these matters of American domestic tranquility. Also Liberty - is the right to act or believe as one person or "various" individuals chooses, and the logic of permission and or authorization - such as within people holding, and or acting in a domestic tranquility format of livable standards. Otherwise a factual concern is recognized when liberty, artificial intelligence, manageable conflicts, and or government control of the American society we live in has a variation of vital corrections with government, societal, and social legislative upgraded values.

Nowadays these changing times are important to control, manage, or discipline anger, and recognize technology issues of liability within numerous concerns. Besides the concept of people with extreme hate similar to Dylann Roof (a white American) who shot 9 black Americans to death during a prayer session at a church in North Carolina is slightly "different" from someone who commits such a crime while hearing voices.

As of hearing voices this was considered the case with Aaron Alexis whom committed mass murders at a U.S. Naval base in Washington D.C., but the "Mixture of Admissibility" evidence of this crisis has been complex for the courts to find admissible "supportive values" of evidence about the prevention of hearing voices. This vital concern and issue should not completely be held as inadmissible without the highest level of formal testimony, and government commitments, arguments, and or understanding to establish technological and social corrections.

The use of different technological systems, and discretionary opinions that can cause occasionally dangerous levels of crime, and negligence leading to harm has added destructive mood altering conflicts. As all artificial intelligence with Illegal and Hazardous Commercial Satellite use consisting of human and more so machinery alterations - various conflicts have become a vital and severe crisis. This crisis concern even has an effect on "Americas infant mortality rate" which has become an increasing and complex problem. Understanding this is a problem that most adults only slightly understand, then therefore as "children are born innocent" without knowledge, it's a fact that their survival is and has become occasionally more difficult. This even includes unwanted infant children being left anyplace on the streets or young children being shot to death by gang violent issues.

The increasing level of tragic fatalities including mass murder's with various conditions of violence, criminal fatal negligence, and confusion has consisted of people occasionally killing mostly other people whom they have never known. Also an increasing concern of terrorism has been part of this equation. Then this level of confusion has spread to young pregnant mothers that don't know or care how they are going to care for their newborn baby's especially without a supportive father, and or income. These are conflicts which resulted in complicated motives, and conditional tragic results similar to Americans and others in well developed countries trying to figure out the anger of Middle East terrorist organizations like ISIL, and ISIS.

Observing the 1990s and the first decade of 2000 numerous regions loss a sense of decency, and respect along with "occupational standards, professional standards, and overall codes of conduct". This was factual apart from destructive gang violence, and how numerous professionals pursued or instigated harm within American corporations like Enron Corporation, WorldCom (c/o MCI), Ameritech Corporation, and various other large and small semi-fraudulent business activities. Then with an enormous amount of new technology America found its self in a mode to better regulate new technology upon which some peoples 1st ambition was to commit acts of crime with technology especially involving sex, and money. This crisis in America caused a low rate of marriage between men and woman - including an enormous rate of bankruptcies.

As numerous businesses like Ameritech Corporation, and WorldCom Corporation had been violating certain complex laws which made other people confused victims, an even higher rate of peoples Constitutional rights were being severely violated. Observing the 1st and 4th Amendments of the U.S. Constitution along with other individual local, state, and federal regulation, various issues within the use of satellites seem to partly be the cause of massive manufacturing explosions. As unlawful commercial satellite use seem to be out of control "one of many" industry fatal explosions occurring during 2005 was at the BP (c/o Amoco and British Petroleum transitioned) Texas City, Texas refinery as it was a tremendous accident that had similarly not occurred over numerous decades. Then 5 years later (2010) the BP Deepwater Horizon oil rig exploded and sank causing a major oil leek lasting 87 days that was the worst of its kind in American history.

Considering the 2005 Texas City, Texas BP refinery explosion "which" was the worse explosion they have had since 1947 is a strange indicator of complacency or "failed artificial intelligence" which had occurred. Observing this factual problem, some people involved in certain communication companies, or close to Ameritech Corporation spent time obtaining information illegally which seem to distract others whom missed vital detailed refinery and or manufacturing procedures within industrial natural gas processes.

Another fatal accident included a natural gas chemical explosion at northern Indiana's Bata Steel plant with gas pipes being extracted with a torch burning process causing a massive explosion. The explosion killed 3 contractors, and injured numerous other employees. This issue within liability and bad liberty caused a lack of sovereignty with some "opinionated or misguided" other people who did not help maintain our domestic tranquility, prosperity, and other lawful or even moral values as part of extensive ongoing disasters.

Within the (1776) creation, and century's of valued amendments of the United States Constitution, along with various Civil Rights activities (c/o the 1960s) involving Martin Luther King the diversified resources of American "Liberty" has established many landmarks. These landmarks of improved liberty and liability have given us a resource of good, occasional bad, and or indifferent values. Also these are values that regulate products, and technology that is a government implementation of responsibility, and duty of value -- similar to the consolidated prohibition of alcohol which is still being regulated after almost 100 years. Considering these alcohol values of being legal to make, manufacture, and sale alcohol, and other potentially hazardous products, regulation is vital for social and public safety conditions of responsible use and discipline.

Understanding the legislative implementation of numerous industries, and technological products like computers and satellites -- these product and service concerns consisting of lawmaking and amendment disciplines of regulatory values will conditionally take just as long as the regulated disciplines of alcohol. These are vital responsibilities, and disciplines along with other potentially hazardous products if we as American's take clear observation of future prosperity. Then this would logically improve the artificial intelligent capacity between human and machinery levels of tolerance. Observing these different forces of human and technology values of regulation, distinct affirmations occasionally must be part of the balance within severely Un-Constitutional conflicts.

Logical and regulated affirmations can reduce the harm or even destruction that unlawful artificial intelligence with computers and more so satellites can conditionally cause. These are factual concerns which have been considered with numerous technology product issues that are created with numerous artificial intelligence programming, communications, and imagery that so many people don't understand how to cope with, or even sometimes tolerate. This can become the disturbances within peoples logical confidentiality, and means of total silence in the commercial airspace which appropriates moral solitude and good decision making.

As the American system of government along with the people have embraced numerous resources of new technology, it must be understood that the people's tolerance will be tested. Their tested tolerance will be vital to adjust to certain conditional results of an advanced format of technology which occasionally is more than they can bare for the most vital good of the overall American society. Observing this a certain amount of mass murders, and domestic murder with occasional suicide including numerous suspected defendants "if they live" have very seldom given a clear motive, or reason for their tragic, and violent acts. This tragic result is factual within the case of Andrea Yates (Texas), Kevin Isom (Gary,

Indiana), and a vast amount others that did live or survive through this level of extreme madness.

If the American society compares domestic murder, terrorist attacks, and lately suicides as diversified fatalities "to the numerous" amount of people killed from gang and gun violence -- most of these diversified fatalities in the courts have still "not" produced a vast amount of logical results for motives. Then unresolved arguments have outpaced our courtroom conditions of motives, and tolerance of domestic murders, and mass murders which even includes infant mortality cases. Also this has included the madness of some woman that have used a baseball bat, other blunt force trauma objects, or even drowning their children to death in bath tubes has become a severe problem, and crisis. Considering this the most innocent of Americans including infant children are being killed for what reason we may have a complex and hard time ever understanding completely why!

Observing the highest rate of suicide during mass murders, numerous differences can be a critical issue within tolerance and a "lack of liberty and or sovereignty". Then various domestic murders ended up with people killing themselves along with others which is a matter of not just a crime of passion between men and woman, but with diversified crimes against society. Observing the lack of sovereignty which leads to a lack of liberty numerous tragedies that are mentally, physically, financially, and then even fatally harmful are sometimes due to the defendants lack of sovereignty, liberty, and liability.

As it has been observed, American woman whom commit violent and various acts of madness within homicide rarely have used a gun to commit mass murders, or most times domestic murder contrary to occasional suicide. This provides the observation that men have been provoked to act aggressively in ways that are more complex, and destructive then most normal times in American history. Therefore the common denominator seems to be a conflicting equation between men and woman as it applies to how they commit these crimes of anger, and the indifferent results that are concerning numerous motives that are extremely complex to explain.

When it applies to satellites and artificial intelligence a vast amount of men, woman, fraternities, sororities, and strangely homosexuals have instigated conflicts between various other men and woman relationships including their planning resources of marriage. One of the most complex investigative evaluations of tragic results with anger have been with the indifference of woman that used a variation of ways to harm or kill their children. Ebony Wilkerson, and Susan Smith committed crimes of anger by driving their vehicles into large bodies of water. These two acts of anger resulted with Susan Smith killing her 2 sons Michael Smith 3 years old, and Alexander Smith 14 months old with them drowning in a South Caroline lake during October of 1994. Then on March 8, 2014 the act of anger within Ebony Wilkerson resulted in her attempting to drive a vehicle with herself, and children into a costal part of the Atlantic Ocean in Florida failed, when she got stuck in deep sand below these coastal waters. Therefore the concept of men apart from woman that commit these acts of madness have very different conclusive results which these acts were similar to Andrea Yates, and a few other woman.

Observing pathological evaluations of violent crimes, and more so financial crimes -- men and woman in government and business are closely and conditionally almost unequal in certain violent and financial violations of law. Contrary to this evaluation more men have been involved in corporate fraud, and woman more so in local government fraud and thief. These financial tragedies contrary to violent crime have destroyed corporations, and various financial matters in local government that will never most times completely be paid back as compensation by the prosecuted defendants. Considering these facts corporations like Enron Corporation, WorldCom Corporation, and various others do not exist anymore. Then numerous amounts of small and large cities and towns (c/o government) have been financially subjected to economic troubles (c/o even bankruptcy filings) has escalated since the 1990s throughout 2013.

Understanding violent, and financial crimes in America has caused a vast amount of people to be victimized with the illogical fact of what to do, and how to solve these massive personal problems have become part of an array of a social crisis. The concept of Illegal and Hazardous Commercial Satellite use being worse than the Watergate crisis has caused extremely difficult problems. Most of these unsolved problems have occurred to peoples personal and small business affairs apart from corporate executives that pay American lawyers extremely well. Therefore the good or even bad service's as it applies to Constitutional law in America is a discretionary issue of liability, risk, and possible diversified reward.

The most common American businesses expanding apart from Illegal and Hazardous Commercial Satellite use have been with "internet and satellite" companies which is most times part of artificial intelligence. Understanding this advanced technology has been conflicting contrary to older and more well established technology applied to corporate businesses having their normal operational, and market values of progress. Otherwise this has become the destructive logic of people that oppose other people's logical effort to live and work at a responsible rate of prosperity as they evaluate the changing times, and technology in America.

Within the logic of Americans becoming confused between domestic tranquility, the good and bad changing times including prosperity apart from tremendous economic disasters, anger, and various levels of grief have occurred. Then it becomes normal if very few complex crimes and conflicts are keeping people from maintaining a valued life style of prosperity due to these good and bad changing times. Understanding this the concept of domestic tranquility becomes a diversified conflict within good, bad, and destructive emotions that sometimes applies to the tolerance of advanced technology that is workable or non-workable upon being properly regulated with logical enforcement. Considering these facts historical disasters, tragedies, and the levels of controlled tolerance within liberty can be understood at a normal rate.

# A SATELLITE AND COMMUNICATION SPECTRUM WORSE THAN THE WATERGATE CRISIS

(14)

## CHAPTER FOURTEEN

(14)

Anger and Technology In America

Worse Than The Watergate Crisis, Without Domestic Tranquility

# A SATELLITE AND COMMUNICATION SPECTRUM WORSE THAN THE WATERGATE CRISIS

(14)

Within the understanding of Americas advancements in technology along with other well developed countries it should be recognized that these changing "technological" times have been part of diversified effects. The main concern of this chapter will outline how America has become occasionally too dependent on satellite and wireless technology, and therefore ignoring certain vital details of reality to normally keep America stable. Also this becomes the logic that these "good and bad" changing times are more advanced and lately complex then the times during the (1970s) with the Watergate scandal, and crisis. Actually with the advancements of satellite, and overall communication spectrum values, Americans must be concerned that there are no destructive or severely unlawful issues concerning this airspace concept of technology.

A vast amount of these comparison issues and evaluation factors between a system and spectrum of satellite, communication, and telecommunication uses are to be applicable to our American system of Constitutional laws. Then the enormous amount of people obtaining information illegally, or instigating destructive conflicts can be managed against a tremendous amount of advanced harm. These are harmful problems which effected the overall American society worse than the effects of the Watergate scandal, and even other similar crisis matters. This is even valued on how the Internet Financial and Business Bubble burst on mostly investors during the early 1990s similar to hundreds of other products and services which were held as good, and bad consumer rated issues or they were ruled, and or determined unfit for society.

Observing various telecommunication, communication, and satellite spectrum activities which should include advanced professional disciplines of legislature these are values of United States Constitutional law. These are vital concerns during these changing technological times in America which goes along with the lawful and safe use of every form of technology. As the 1972 and 1973 Watergate legal crisis was tremendous to the American system of government, similar problems (c/o technology) has been a consistent review of legislative revisions of these historical conflicts or conditions. Then this becomes the critical conflict to the American people, and our somewhat considered well developed society which seems to have endured more fatalities, and financial problems along with crimes then most times in American history.

Considering the changing times, various conflicts and a "lack of enforced law disciplines" most times includes duties by the Federal Communication Commission (FCC), and the Federal Trade Commission (FTC) which becomes the logic of why so many people have been forced into extremely complex and overall crimes. Contrary to financial crimes a tremendous amount of acts within violence has been questionable as it is applied to anger, and economic hardships. So as it applies to the FCC, and the FTC their regulatory base of enforcing the airspace spectrum laws apply to the Constitution which have been at an all-time destructive or inefficient low rate. Basically good regulation is not keeping up with the harmful effects of some considerably bad or "unconstitutional technology" that is advanced in the American society we live.

The FCC and the FTC legal conflicts which become the unlawful logic that spying and conspiracy in its many forms in Washington D.C. (c/o similar Watergate type crimes) and now in all other American states lately is causing diversified harm. These conditions of harm are against relationships between man and woman (c/o marriage), numerous financial conflicts disrupting retirement savings, investments, and income which in diversified conflicts includes various unlawful excessive fines or fees, and even fatal violent crimes. Otherwise the satellite and overall technology spectrum consist of people with good, bad, and indifferent ideas that are occasionally dangerously unlawful.

An American society along with inefficient regulations for technology in the United States is and has become a severe problem and crisis which seem to be instigating mass murders. This issue of mass murders or domestic murder with occasional suicide is a tremendous problem even with the spoken word, actions, and observation of President Barack Obama. Considering this, millions of American people observe the needs of this crisis to be corrected similar to corrections that were made after the Great Depression in America during the 1930s. Then even comparing the many recalls lately in the automobile industry, or arguments about gun control we seem to never here of satellite or any form of telecommunication, and or communication recalls or logical corrections that at least are mentally harmful. There have been a few class actions law suits over guns, and vehicles with very few legal corrections similar to the news stories about the Watergate scandal years ago and how it applies to communication.

When a national society of legal scholars or diversified professionals like doctors or engineers are restricted or intimidated by various legal proceedings the American society is subjected to be treated any way some large companies (c/o bad individuals or government) want to instigate harm. Therefore besides AT&T and more so their subsidiaries like the former Ameritech Corp, various Amateur and Professional satellite and or radio activist or service providers must be retrained with disciplinary actions, and or prosecution. Also this includes companies like BP, Raytheon Corporation, Google, various others including foreign communication businesses, or even valued corporations like ExxonMobile and General Electric as the American people still have lawful rights to be protected against various corporate law violations, crimes, and or negligence.

Understanding the numerous corporate businesses that create, and provide operational disciplines of technology that are somewhat highly inadmissible un-affirmed conflicts can be a destructive distraction. These destructive issues of technology within satellites, and some telecommunication activity can cause various conflicts that have not been considered in the courts similar to the Watergate hearings. This vitally includes issues of why America fought the Vietnam War applicable to humanitarian support. Observing this communications, satellites, and as it applies to the defense of the United States has various vital matters of importance which has been unobserved until total disaster similar to the "After Mass" of Hurricane Katrina, numerous fatal manufacturing explosions (1995 to 2008), and the September 11, 2001 terrorist attacks.

Considering its obvious why we as Americans went to war after the September 11, 2001 terrorist attacks due to clear evidence, it is also extremely clear that our advanced technology and officials within the United States government failed miserably. Also Hurricane Katrina during 2005 was a tremendous failure (contrary to effective predictions) with the after mass damage conditionally that could have been prevented. After severe criticism and the prosecution of former New Orleans Mayor Ray Nagin very few effective laws have been crated apart from rebuilding the levees, and numerous other infrastructure projects.

Observing the 9-11 Report attacks, Hurricane Katrina, and many other issues of failure has become the good, and bad of American technology concerning the "Best Lawful" uses possible. America has been considered one of the most well developed countries in the world upon which less advanced nations, and countries with terrorist that hate America have been able to apply and cause extensive harm to various parts of the United States. A factual comparison of this problem also exist of how the American society victimizes its own people which sometimes includes the bewilderment of why have so many of these bazaar incidents like mass murders or numerous domestic murder have all a sudden started happing at rational rates.

The September 11, 2001 terrorist attacks being a critical problem of Anti-Americans full of hate is stated with observed intelligence about the people America did not stop from harming 1000s of Americans and causing billions of dollars of asset damage. These are vital issues which is described in the U.S. federal government's 9-11 Report after this tragedy. Considering these facts including the establishment of the Department of Homeland Security during the President George Bush Jr. administration, America increased its budget items enormously for extra security, and defense. Then as terrorism is a worldwide issue with numerous attacks, the United States has hopefully set logical standards that will eradicate numerous problems.

Observing government duties and problems the United States was not a stranger to international crimes against the U.S. like terrorist high-jacking airplanes during the 1970s and 1980s as things had sadly got bad or worse within the changing times. Then the 1st terrorist bombing of the New York World Trade Center in 1993 was by 4 middle eastern men with the last names of Abouhalima, Ajaj, Ayyad, and Salameh as the United States was still un-alert until September 11, 2001. Therefore with numerous people including William Daly working for Ameritech Corp, and then the Department of Commerce as of him using Illegal and Hazardous Commercial Satellites against innocent Americans, and small business owners he and other government and business officials neglected to detect or stop this disastrous attack.

Contrary to my own (J. Reeves) issues, problems, and concerns I observed William Daly and a number of other people between Northwest Indiana, and Northeast Illinois instigating conflicts against Americans causing mental, and financial destruction. The major damage they done and pursued was working to destroy small local (Gary & other cities) American owned businesses, and family values. Then these businesses were replaced with an enormous amount of middle eastern business owners. Therefore between him and other people close to the Nation of Islam it seems that they ruined businesses, and supported an Enemy Foreign Agenda all from mostly Illegal & Hazardous Commercial Satellite Use, and "then again like the 70s and 80s high-jacked airplanes" resurfaced.

From the 1970s to the 2000s numerous good, and bad satellite, communication, and telecommunication issues were active (in all states) accept for American's not being ready to defend the country from the 9-11 Report attacks. Contrary to these facts in the 1990s and 2000s Americans were becoming a culture of angry people especially those victimized by Illegal and Hazardous Commercial Satellite use causing them mental distractions from hearing voices. Then as Americans went through an anger crisis again similar to the 1930s after World War I, and the 1929 stock market crash causing the Great Depression with a Run on the Nation's Banks - stability became hard for various people to observe or maintain. Then the Vietnam War of the 1960s and 1970s including an Energy crisis with extremely long lines at the gas pumps was agonizing for millions of people at gas stations throughout the United States. Otherwise years later, extra laws and departments like the U.S. Department of Energy were established and this became an increased regulatory value were the satellite spectrum also becomes an active crisis and regulatory concern.

Numerous issues of technology advancing was observed by the United States government similar to energy, transportation, and communications industries making advancements with occasional caution. The Communications Satellite Act was passed by Congress in 1962 which specified that private corporations be created to develop "a" communication satellite system. The Communications Satellite Act of 1962 limited the U.S. government's role in various organizations that operate as a business resource within the media, and therefore other government powers were given to the Federal Trade Commission (FTC) to enforce certain media activities. These FTC duties and powers were to protect people like writers of books, magazines, and movies so their work was secured from thief along with their Copyrights, and to protect citizens from unlawful practices in radio and television communications including advertising, and indecency.

The FCC over the decades have had the duty to assign radio and television frequencies, but today satellite frequencies have been un-responded to without regulatory adjustments. Between the FCC, the FTC and even the somewhat confidentiality of the Securities and Exchange Commission (SEC) a crisis has evolved in all these resources of government and more. These and other government concerns are vitally guarded under the U.S. Constitution, and the Constitution of all individual state governments to protect the people and society. Then when some commercial satellite issues become a mental, physical, financial, and fatal resource of harmful frequencies that violate all Constitutional laws possible, an extensive amount of problems becomes an expanding crisis.

As more satellites have been sent into orbit over the last 5 decades and any land based satellites this has created what's considered satellite (space) junk on earth and especially in the outer space of orbit. These satellites concerning access within lawful, unlawful or indifferent conflicts should be reviewed and evaluated for information collection and resources of manageable affirmations. Otherwise these possible resources of dangerous, hazardous, and expensive products being unattended to without solutions by the National Aeronautics and Space Administration (NASA) officials, other responsible government officials, and various corporations becomes an increasing problem. This is the conflict of them having established a backlog, and crowed atmosphere of satellites which we can only understand that maybe a solution is being considered to these "advanced technology crisis concerns".

Understanding the crowed atmosphere of satellites and satellite communication systems observed in and by the United States have serviced many good, bad, conflicting, and disastrous issues as an appropriate level of legislative and judicial work has to be considered. A logical observation, and workable value for wireless and satellite systems exist within the legislative actions that "The More Technology we have - the More Regulation we more than likely Need". Occasionally these become values of prompt decision making by government when society recognizes that American people are suffering, and don't know what to do to have a normal life. Therefore the equation of human (man or woman) VS machinery (c/o satellites) is factored with artificial intelligence concerns that need to be corrected with revisions to active frequencies in the commercial airspace.

Logical regulation is an active concern in a vast amount of corporate public, private businesses or occasional government resources. This concern of satellite regulation also goes along the value of U.S. Satellite defense systems which is vitally important against foreign enemies. Also this is vitally important in weather satellites, and aviation satellites that has created value and resourceful comfort for the American society. Then any negative activity from old or new satellite systems against American citizens, and their neurological existence can be tremendously complex, and disastrous upon how it has even made America vulnerable if we are not careful. Since the 1990s America and its technology has occasionally been vulnerable to "International Investments with International Terror", adding to the long term existence of "U.S. domestic crimes, conflicts, and disasters".

Observing international investments that include international terror, government officials in Chicago, Il discovered that after the September 11, 2001 attacks that certain Illinois Islamic organizations wear sending ($100,000s) hundreds of thousands of dollars back to the Middle East to fight against American troops. These are critical federal violations of law against the United States (c/o people, assets, and other concerns) during a time of war.

As some Americans were forced out of work, and or their businesses this became a failing conflict strangely including Illegal and Hazardous Commercial Satellite Use as more money started flowing into the hands of people supporting Middle East terrorist or even domestic criminal enterprises. Then apart from those long time American businesses that supported American values, step by step tragedies reoccurred. These were American small business owners that took serious losses keeping them from supporting people, and issues in their communities. Then various organizations like Little League Baseball, Ballet, numerous other activities for the youth, and sometimes senior citizens that need help were left out of the equation of prosperity as well the business owners whom had to abandon various plans for any business expansion.

Apart from the discretionary business survival for born in America business owners an enormous concept of publicity during the Watergate crisis is similar to the arguments discussed about government surveillance observing after the September 11, 2001 attacks which applies to wiretapping and satellite uses. These government issues were established as the Foreign Intelligence Surveillance Act of 1978 which conditionally established the National Security Agency (NSA). The NSA consisted of a "Warrantless Surveillance" program of extensive activities observed during 2001 to 2007 which was the question of concern by numerous people and various large corporations. Considering these complex facts any unlawful surveillance observing some activity between 1991 and September 11, 2001 consisted of various people in corporations (c/o Ameritech) and the government needing to outline and correct the fact that they did not know or understand the conclusive extent of this technology. This becomes somewhat insecure - almost like some law enforcement officials (c/o their Swearing In) that applies to their actions under state and federal Constitutional laws.

Unlawful surveillance against Americans with an immigration crisis (c/o the 1990s & 2000s) as it applies to the American system of government became harmful to citizens born in America. Opponents have argued and discretionally support numerous foreign people to say they are the real builders and developers of America, but they seem to forget or failed to understand that the Mexican American War (1846-1847), was fought right before the Civil War in America (1861-1865), and World War's I & II including numerous other issues with spy's and conflicts were problems. Even today, looking back on the Revolutionary War (1775-1783) America (c/o of a Government) and England (c/o a Parliament) there are conflicting differences of opinions within the people, and various social values contrary to being allies. Therefore we in America must be careful how we support allies or enemies that lately has become out of control, especially when our nation (the U.S.) destroys its own people with technology, and foreign people will occasionally do the same and sometimes worse to Americans.

# PEOPLE TO HEAR VOICES IN THE COMMERCIAL AIRSPACE

(15)

# CHAPTER FIFTEEN

(15)

Anger and Technology In America

Worse Than The Watergate Crisis, Without Domestic Tranquility

# PEOPLE TO HEAR VOICES IN THE COMMERCIAL AIRSPACE

(15)

A critical problem, and crisis that seems to have began in the 1970s, and then up to the 1990s throughout the year 2016 and hopefully not the future - has been American people Neurologically hearing voices in the commercial airspace. This is a problem that can be determined to come from Americas problematic Commercial Airspace with unlawful or destructive satellite activities which includes equipment that is being used by individuals, corporations, and sometimes even government. As it may be observed these are the types of neurological distractions that will more than likely create anger more than happiness or other diversified conflicts within livable human emotions. Then as it may be observed that any external forces can penetrate or reach parts of the human anatomy (c/o the internal nerve or neurological system) such as with active satellite technology this can cause mental, physical, financial, and even fatal harm.

Observing that commercial satellites can cause a lake of full sovereignty which is part of mental, physical, financial, and fatal distractions a tremendous crisis has developed. Considering these concerns the American society of advanced technology with lawful and unlawful commercial satellites (c/o hearing voices of conflicting opinions) becomes the equation of more anger. This level of anger has instigated an enormous amount of people to commit some of the worse crimes of violence that Americans have ever seen, and or endured as a crisis. Otherwise this has occurred more than most times then ever during the 1990s, and the 1st decade of the 2000s exceeding other tragedies throughout the history of the United States. Then our American society of government is severely mixed on what to do to solve this problem that has reached crisis level concerns.

Considering the issue that a vast amount of people commit "complex to understand crimes" lately in America - this is usually factored with them uncontrollably hearing voices. These voice transmitted frequencies sometimes can be detected, and sometimes can not be detected by the people being effected. Some peoples voices that are heard in commercial space are most times using commercial satellites which may be in the form of Google Earth or other satellite programmed operating technology by government and or businesses, while other people, who's voices are being heard are not always extremely complex "if a person understands communication satellite frequencies".

The rate of people overall that here voices in the commercial airspace is even larger without some people committing extreme acts of violence, but a vast amount of people do seek mental health treatment services that consist of a high medical cost if they are uninsured. This being a serious crisis a Republican Presidential candidate Donald Trump (during campaigning in 2015) stated that we "In America" have a tremendous mental health problem. Contrary to Democrats or Republicans its always somewhat interesting to outline this mental health crisis, but what is causing it, and how to solve the problem becomes the governments legislative and judicial priority (c/o any executive orders).

The statements made by Donald Trump, and a vast amount of others including President Barack Obama was based on rapid and extensive occasions of violent gun activity in America. During the Barack Obama administration he has had to witness and evaluate mass murders (c/o fatal shootings) with guns at least 7 major critical times in different parts of America. This especially applies to the unlawful use of guns with enormous amounts of ammunition, and that have fully automatic firing capabilities with some people angry and or hearing voices - besides gang violence. Therefore this lawful and unlawful gun use issue, consist of various mental health concerns, and our American diversified resource of technology which is part of a destructive condition within an increase of people committing unexplainable violent crimes.

The discrete argument lately between gun violence, mental health, and technology has been somewhat tremendous. One of the main factors of concern is the U.S. Constitution's 2nd Amendment, but a vast amount of Americans fail to look closer at how technology has changed the 1st, 2nd, 4th, and other Amendments of the Constitution. Considering Constitutional law and the abundance of laws that are occasionally a sense of executive orders by various presidents, there are U.S. Court Martial laws that are rarely argued or they have not been argued with a logical since of publicity that apply to commercial satellites. Considering this crisis within diversified laws it applies to all other regulatory legal disciplines under the U.S. Constitution. Then this becomes a conflicting factor to instigate people to be angry, violent, or even more so depressed about various conflicts including any critical financial and economic levels of uncontrolled insecurity.

Contrary to discretionary arguments in the courts these facts of violence with very few motives consist of a certain amount of people that had some form of wealth. These were people like Adam Lanza (c/o the Sandy Hook Elementary School shooting 2012), James Holmes (the Aurora, Colorado movie theater shooter 2012), Aaron Alexis (the Washington D.C. Naval Yard shooter 2013), the two Columbine (1999) shooters, and the 2007 Virginia Tech shooting (c/o 31 dead) committed by Seung-Hui-Cho upon which these people did not seem to be poor people, or were they anywhere near becoming homeless. This is similar to some well off people, or people with government authority that occasionally have access to commercial satellites (c/o good & bad usage), and other resources of technology with financial support.

Various people that were not super rich, or wealthy, but they had the potential to live a somewhat comfortable life, seem to be trapped in this Endless Loop crisis of "anger and or hearing voices". On the other hand certain people had financial hardships that were not nationally known like Kevin Isom of Gary, Indiana whom killed his wife and 2 stepchildren as he was unemployed. Then as a former security guard he had a vast amount of guns, but did not go out and commit a crime like armed robbery. Also Angelica Alvarez of Goshen, Indiana was having financial troubles while she was separated from her husband, as she then drowned her 4 children to death. These disasters constantly were locally tragic to various communities, but others became an issue of national concern as the overall economy has been sluggish.

As I believe the human conscience mind within thinking and decision making was loss in some ways with various people, various domestic murders, and mass murders became worse with non-criminal minded people. In terms of another person who fell into financial hardships was Lukesha Holloway whom at 24 years old was living in her car with her 3 year old daughter before she decided to crash her car into a crowd of people on the Las Vegas strip. Within the fact that 1 person died instantly, and 31 other people were injured, her state of mind (diversely) goes back to the level of depression that some people "suffered with" during the 1929 stock market crash, and run on banks. Then the mix of satellite issues (c/o possibly hearing voices) and other conflicts becomes part of mental and financial harm that is tremendous to resolve. These are facts about diversified citizens of America that seem to have no logical motive for their fatally or deadly violent use of guns or other objects (c/o occasional suicide) as frustration causes these acts of violence, and conflicting anger.

Understanding the American society of political ambition a vast amount of Republicans similar to Congressman Paul Ryan, and others (c/o also Democrats) whom support the values of the 2$^{nd}$ Amendment had made some gun use and violence issues a critical, and or conflicting concern. Considering Congressman Paul Ryan has been valuable in the American system of government all Republicans, and Democrats have not found a solution to this problem which includes gun legislation that is "truly not or clearly not" the only answer to this "Endless Loop Crisis" as some people have admitted. Then therefore as technology is considered in America we somewhat let it be part of our unconcerned human nature of whether certain satellite technology is good or bad and how it is used effecting American people who lawfully own guns.

As a few members of the U.S. Congress have argued some concerns about the 1$^{st}$ and 4$^{th}$ Amendments of the United States Constitution and some issues of technology - admissible satellite activities (c/o inadmissibility) are complex for them to outline or prove. Then to connect these factors to various commercial satellite activity, and any destructive interference on people's lives has been impartial contrary to the increase in mass murders or people hearing instigating voice communication transmissions. The closest that the U.S. Congress has argued this is more so within the Patriot Act, and the National Security Agency (NSA) "warrant-less" surveillance activity which has increased sense the 9-11 Report terrorist attacks. Otherwise before the 9-11 Attacks the American system of government was not just seeking terrorist, and even the logical use of satellites besides tapping telephone lines as this was a broader problem for a vast amount of innocent American citizens. This was a critical concern (c/o some Americans supporting an Enemy Foreign Agenda) causing a vast amount of law bidding citizens to become misguided, being arrested, victimized upon occasionally being forced into anger, and even shot and or killed along with other possible conflicts.

Observing guns and mental health discrepancies have increased, more people hearing commercial airspace voices in numerous regions of America consist of conflicts which have gotten out of control. These issues have consisted of the financial wellbeing of American's to own or buy guns, which has consisted of some people who have seem to lose a sense of appropriate judgment. The format of bad judgment seems to be part of manipulated conflicts upon instigating people to become angry or misguided about a series of events, and or conflicts. This is considered by the instigated and unauthorized words of other people, inappropriate law enforcement, political government conflicts and or other concerns of trying to dictate various people. Then upon the broadening logic of various conflicts that have evolved in a relevant factor of how some mass murders are various peoples 1st, and only violent crime, these mentally or financially troubled conflicts effected people (c/o being victimized and then defendants) to commit numerous types of crime. Otherwise America is and may be losing potentially good people.

James Holmes (the Colorado movie theater shooter) during the 1990s and going into the 1st decade of 2000 was a person whom was becoming more difficult to understand by his well off family (even as he is a college graduate). His father as a university mathematician, and his mother a nurse is a logical fact for him growing up in a well off home. Also he grew up during a time of expanding artificial intelligence (c/o even movies), expanding cell phone use, internet with satellites, extensive gun violence by gangs, and various other tragedies. These are tragedies occasionally by conflicting businesses, government, and or individuals that more so instigate apparent destructive problems, and that did not help prevent a certain amount of disasters that have recently occurred. In light of this James Holmes even had resourceful money to buy a Batman character custom (Dark Vader) and numerous guns before committing this violent rampage, and conspiracy of a fatal shooting at a Colorado movie theater. Therefore his mental state of decision making and conscience thinking (between California and Colorado) loss judgment and conscience observation on how to live in a civil society.

A similar financial concern within a well off household consisted of Adam Lanza who's father is a corporate executive that left his divorced wife Nancy Lanza with a comfortable means of alimony, which appropriated the fact that she did not need to work. Considering this, Nancy Lanza whom was killed by her son Adam during this terrible (Sandy Hook) event, also spent an enormous amount of money and time on her enthusiastic passion for guns including regular visits to local shooting ranges. Adam Lanza and his brother were included in these visits to shooting ranges which was part of their regular life. Then observing their passion for guns and shooting explains Adam's knowledge to use various guns, and have good accuracy. Otherwise the guns that were used at Sandy Hook had been purchased, and owned lawfully, and before and during this deadly shooting - sometimes a person hears voices, but they will not tell other people, or conditionally they do not understand what to do to correct this problem.

Correcting a problem within people who hear voices has been a complex issue that even people in the medical profession have trouble correcting this so called diagnoses issue. This is based on the consideration of "if the medical industry and profession can ever find a logical solution" which more so applies to the values of satellite technological industry disciplines. In the same concern thousands of people in America and throughout the world quit drinking alcohol, smoking cigarettes, and or using illegal drugs, but people that hear satellite voices have an enormously hard time eliminating the voices that they hear. Then as these people are sometimes considered crazy, or mentally ill, the conflict of who too trust, and how to discuss these concerns becomes a tremendous evaluation.

As most people who hear voices, this is not a basic issue of just common sense. This is "totally uncommon", and it seems to be increasing rapidly as it somewhat becomes more complex to some of the smartest people in America. This is a concern along with peoples intellectual thinking, and decision making, but government seems to not want to correct this crisis, or maybe pay settlements through the courts for these extensive damages, and more than likely be accused of violating executive orders. Another factor has been how a certain amount of relationships and marriages between men and woman have been destroyed. This includes some cities having an extremely low rate of marriages that is somewhat considered lately as being at historical crisis levels. Therefore people have a complex time understanding each other.

The American medical industry is aggressively pursuing financial gains like other professions, but this problem of "Hearing Voices" due to "Illegal and Hazardous Commercial Satellite Use" is more than a medical problem, or illness. Even as many Americans have stated that we have a crisis within mental health, they conditionally do not mention or say - "we as Americans may have a commercial airspace and satellite problem" that is out of control. This becomes similar to the issues that were ignored which then became tragedies like Hurricane Katrina with the New Orleans levees collapsing (2005). Then numerous fatal manufacturing explosions including the Texas City, Texas BP explosion (2005), and various others in Indiana, Illinois, Wisconsin, North Carolina, and other states on the east coast of the United States.

Various tragic accidents (c/o explosions) occurred in Indiana at Bata Steel, in North Carolina - at Synthron Inc., in Milwaukee, Wisconsin at Falk Corporation, and others upon which sometimes people hearing voices can be critically mistaken, or cause mistakes, disturbances, and or distractions. This Indiana incident got to the extreme point of contract workers forgetting that the gas was on in a gas pipe upon which 3 workers were killed as they began using an extraction torch that caused an explosion. Even in Chicago, Illinois digging to close to some underground gas pipes were ruptured by heavy duty construction tools causing a small explosion, and a quickly expanding fire. This gets to the point of extreme distraction or incompetence. Then considering various types of explosions that occurred in a few different places, and times is part of making bad and repetitious mistakes. Contrary to the fact, people commonly make mistakes or on occasions dangerous errors, but over and over again becomes an extensive problem.

So as mental health is a problem - numerous fatal accidents or madness at record rates have also been just as bad as mass murders, or issues like the explosion that Timothy McVeigh caused to destroy the Alfred P Murrah Federal building during 1995. Even though there were 3 other conspiring accomplishes with him which included his old U.S. Army buddy Terry Nichols this tragedy seem to set off continuous madness throughout the United States. This even includes the madness of increasing gang violence in various parts of America considering more people were going through expanding mental health concerns.

Another sense of madness was displayed by John Allen Muhammad whom was convicted of capital murder and executed in November of 2009 for him being considered and outlined as the Beltway Sniper. His accomplish Lee Boyd Malvo whom was 17 years old at the time when they conspired to shoot and killed 10 people, and injured 3 others with a hidden high powered rifle. John Allen Muhammad's madness was like a number of others in angry custody disputes as he even kidnapped his children at one point along with his admirations of Osama bin Laden and al Qaeda which included his involvement in the Nation of Islam. These are conflicts that occurred after he was honorably discharged from the U.S. Army after 17 years of service. Then in his mental condition whether he was hearing voices or not a vast amount of his anger was terrifying the northeast of the United States with anger to kill other Americans.

# BUSINESS, MONEY, TECHNOLOGY, AND ANGER

## (16)

# CHAPTER SIXTEEN

## (16)

Anger and Technology In America

Worse Than The Watergate Crisis, Without Domestic Tranquility

# BUSINESS, MONEY, TECHNOLOGY, AND ANGER

(16)

The concept of anger and technology surrounding business, and money in America becomes a tremendous discrepancy that increases the indifference of peoples survival mostly to the point of a numerous amount of Americans recently living well, or even sadly being homeless. This even goes along the values of professional codes of conduct, and human relations for citizens, businesses, church establishments, and various people to have opportunities along with domestic tranquility. Then this even outlines how bad businesses or wealthy individuals have to be prosecuted for complex illegal activities.

Considering all businesses are not bad, this most times consist of a good amount of American citizens that depend on their employers - observing these people have a logical and or a secured job as they are employees whom hope they are working for a responsible and secured business. An appropriate example is the good, and bad of small and some large businesses that failed like the former WorldCom Corporation, Montgomery Ward's Corporation, Bear Stearns Investments, Enron Corporation, the Bernie Madoff scandal, and many other diversified issues of business concerns.

Considering numerous economic concerns, various levels of future business evaluations that includes or consist of anger has been part of laid off employees whom become occasionally angry. These are people who have slightly different concerns apart from people that have suffered in a vast amount of diversified ways or conditions upon which anger became a tragic issue. Otherwise business, money, and technology apart from uncorrected government oversights with various issues can cause anger, and is part of America losing a high level of social standards and "domestic tranquility".

Various employers whom sometimes consist of one or more business owners must be legally fair to themselves, their employees, and the communities (c/o state governments) in which they conduct their business. This also goes along the concern of their compliance within the state and federal Constitutions of our American society, and various other laws. Then this is valued along the concern of businesses, individuals, and sometimes government resources that think only about the money, and don't care too much about their products, services, customers, duties, and or the citizens they may harm. As this becomes the logic of admissible and inadmissible evidence a coal mining or automobile accident becomes clearly admissible, but cyber space, and satellite crimes are highly inadmissible until certain factual problems in financial mismanagement, severe negligence, or other criminal conflicts are determined.

In frustrated times, some people would occasionally say money is the root of all evil, but money is not completely evil compared to various peoples ways of respectfully seeking secured financial values or coming into diversified wealth. This has taken years and decades to observe as various parts of the Endless Loop Crisis, and its legal exposure with peoples determination to live good lives or have logical ways of survival and living are part of legal affirmations. Understanding these satellite factors people should be able to have various necessities, or what they need to know along with logical confidentiality which should exist in America. These are factors which are still incomplete with supposedly good people that violate various Constitutional Law Amendments.

When various people are concerned about certain businesses, and individuals that are violating state and federal infractions of law this becomes a crisis concern. This distinctly applies to the United States Constitution upon becoming a misguided issue apart from logical living. Then the concept of numerous legal infractions is part of disciplines that certain people like William Daly of Ameritech Corporation, and others usually did not get certain issues right in public or private business and even thru government. Otherwise with a certain amount of positive public, private business or government duties including some complex issues that did not become part of accomplished goals or values the American people suffered.

The observed insecurity of WorldCom Corp with Bernard Ebbers was an "Anti-Trust" law concern similar to Ameritech Corporation with William Daly which became part of divesture (c/o AT&T) along with some people at all levels of government in various states. Observing this concern one factor is that during William Daly's tenure at Ameritech, and the U.S. Department of Commerce more Congressman and federal government officials died in plane crashes, and other accidents (contrary to the Pentagon and World Trade Centers attack on 9-11-2001) then most 2 to 4 year political spans in American history. These were officials like U.S. Commerce Secretary Ron Brown with various staff members, and a few of his business constituents dying in an airplane crash, Congressman Mickey Leland (dying in an airplane crash), and Congressman Sonny Bono in a skiing accident.

During a rational length of time during William Daly's corporate and government tenure numerous government officials embezzled large amounts of money, and or violated numerous law infractions of our diversified American society. These issues even included violations of high level executive orders of law which made our American society dangerous, and unstable. Also this includes a vast amount of other people creating a severe lack of "domestic tranquility" which becomes a society of non-peaceful unrest that is totally an insecure standard of living. Therefore as this has lingered on up to now 2016 from 1990 the city of Chicago and certain mid-west cities and towns can not easily control the extreme violence, most high rates of homicide, shootings with severe injuries, and numerous murders of young sometimes innocent people in a self-destructive society.

Most issues of injustice have been so bad that, numerous American school districts have had to close hundreds and or thousands of schools nationally. Throughout Gary, Indiana 50% of the schools closed, and in Detroit, Michigan more than 46% of the schools closed. This also includes parts of New Orleans, Chicago, and New Jersey in similar ways which has caused an overall education budget, and financial crisis. Observing these school closure combinations of more than or near 50% becomes tremendous to various city or town school districts, and the communities within the establishment of people and certain economic values. Therefore America during the 1ˢᵗ and 2ⁿᵈ decades the 2000 millennium has become a distraction in many ways concerning education from the 1ˢᵗ grade to all the higher collage and university scholastic level of ranking.

As anger has increased with additional concerns a majority of wealthy people were coming into more wealth apart from those being prosecuted for crimes of greed. Then as more cell phones, internet activity, satellites with radio activity, and diversified computer technology business issues have expanded the rate of overall businesses that have declined. Contrary to numerous products, these issues go along with the advancements of commercial satellite services which "both becomes interesting and conditionally dangerous" to the American society. Then the American society has indecisive concerns within moving cautiously and discretionarily forward as various companies potentially earned billions of dollars lately which increases their asset value, but homelessness and secured employment is a major problem. Contrary to this fact certain research has outlined that over the last 25 to 30 years (c/o 2016) less American entrepreneurs (c/o a reduction of nearly 50%) are creating new businesses.

Apart from various product and service advancements, numerous technological products are offered in various markets, or they are illegally sold to occasionally very bad or insecure people. Most technology issues of extreme concerns, includes the cause of a number of diversified American people who are finding themselves in financial and economic difficulties. This is the uniformed discipline of when technology is not simple to understand or is considered (supposedly) too complex to argue or debate in government along with the proper courts. Therefore a valued format between technology and human resource values must be observed as natural standards. If natural standards don't occur even as one of the few companies other than Ameritech Corp consisting of similar anti-trust law violations was at Quest Communication Corporation most American smaller or potential businesses have and will continue to suffer.

As Americans we must recognize when most defected or conflicting products cause issues of dangerous liability. These also are issues within not being a new or improved older product or service with hopeful values that do not become a technology problem of massive discretionary destruction. Therefore lawfully affirmed products or services can be effective unless used unlawfully, or at a rate of improper discipline. Then as certain technological products started off expensive, but sometimes interesting government and citizen oversight becomes vital. Otherwise they lawfully required product revisions, technology oversight requirements by government, and legislative changes that can become vital amendments of regulative and or legal operating disciplines.

As a vast amount of people feel a need to take discretionary advantage of certain resources of technology this means legal enforcement becomes vital. This is similar to the arbitrary legal values of computer programs, and internet activity for considered legislature or valued laws. So within this evaluation the "more people" that find a use for various technology, the "more we find people" that are willing to use these advanced systems of technology illegally, and then regulatory enforcement is vital to get right.

Understanding the format of a capitalist society, the concentration of economic and financial progress in business is a responsible way of life. This consist of when businesspeople are active and resourceful in conducting business and then the rate of survival is vitally important. Considering this Americans and a diversified amount of people from other countries go into business in America to earn money as a lawful living, but sometimes there is greed, and discretionary business that causes divested value. These are issues similar to thousands of people like Rap artist M.C. Hammer (Stanley Burrell), or as well even developer Donald Trump, and numerous Americans who filed bankruptcy and loss enormous amounts of wealth. Considering these and numerous other people that filed bankruptcy, their economic condition has been considered discretionary value, but usually these are occasionally helpful people, and or they are not always harmful people to America as these financial issues require tremendous corrections.

Observing business and money diversions, certain conflicts have effected various people in negative way's that is Unconstitutionally insecure. This is the distraction of issues which is sometimes causing more conflicts than some people can bare, and then anger dictates. Considering this, numerous people, and businesses throughout various industries with certain values of technology sometimes cause harm to innocent, or troubled people in diversified ways effecting a massive amount of people. These are people whom find themselves trying to make good or appropriate decisions, but are constantly distracted by voices in the commercial airspace, or other conflicts. Then an increase in mass murders have seem to become part of people being pushed away from good decision making, upon which various people became destructive by artificial intelligence.

As tremendous conflicts within a technological capacity becomes an issue, various responsible laws that are not created or enforced become an increasing problem. This is the concern of Americas complex technological changing times which occasionally people become severely troubled. Understanding the laws that are not observed and or otherwise not enforced properly by prosecutors, and the courts with secured budgets is part of unbalanced issues of "wealth and anything goes" in America. Then this becomes a vital subject as hopefully the right decisions are made by government as sometimes they don't care what the people say or what they are suffering through. This is factual to be worse than the Watergate scandal of the early 1970s - especially for the "government money" that was appropriated to solve legal problems, and how this effects small business owners, and numerous citizens.

As anger is determined in many ways, it sometimes has levels of emotions which can be factored from various issues. These are issues such as the loss or disagreements concerning business, employment, family or romantic relationship matters, bankrupt business issues, bankrupt local governments, and also people or businesses trying to survive a massive conflict. An enormous amount of overall conflicts have included the trillions of dollars spent on the September 11, 2001 terrorist attacks, Hurricane Katrina, Hurricane Ike, and numerous other major disasters in various regions of the United States. Otherwise this usually consist of people that try to dictate other people unlawfully instead of proper, and or efficient managing of business values, and social values from hopeful government solutions.

Numerous mistakes, with various fatalities was slightly observed, and ignored when people started sending text massage's on cell phones while driving or operating diversified heavy machinery equipment. This included diversified equipped vehicle's such as trains, boats, semi-trucks, and other public transportation vehicles. Then this has lately become one of the major distractions, and dangers while driving, and or even operating vehicles on public roadways, railroads, seaways, and or in the commercial airspace which new legislature is occasionally (but not good enough) being considered. These issues therefore consist of mental, physical, financial, and fatal harm "due to extensive negligence and or harmful conflicts".

Understanding technological products, and other advanced product or service factors, it's not a new government oversight issue that we endure various advanced products that have occasional unknown results to the American society. Otherwise as these products have generated billions and trillions of dollars throughout the American society, a legislative format of regulation becomes the equation to keep the American general public safe, and even financially secure. Considering this, numerous violations and conflicts can be avoided if instigated harm, and discretionary crime is not a complex inadmissible deterrent.

Observing that the issue of money, massive business, and technology has driven a vast amount of people into the computer, cell phone, and internet sectors of business, Americas issue of technology oversight throughout government and society has established legislative expanded needs. These have become lucrative business opportunities with companies like Apple Computer, Microsoft Corp, Google (Earth), GE Corp., IBM, and Intelsat. Otherwise their extensive cell phone, diverse computer systems, and or satellite products and or useable sales are a logical part of prosperity. This vitally includes each new IPhone, and various other products connected to large computer server systems for tablets, desktop, and laptop computers to communicate with other systems as satellite systems are a vital part of this network. Understanding this, satellites tend to be a bit more complex then these other items.

Considering companies like Microsoft Corporation, Apple Computer, General Electric Corp, AT&T, and International Business Machines (IBM) including most T.V., Radio, and industry values of multi-billion dollar resources of technology these businesses become part of valued brand names. Then their regulatory standards must apply safe operating standards of liability for all Americans. These corporate products and services usually are part of networking systems connected to advanced satellite, software, and hardware computer operating business systems that are a financial and economic subject of valued interest. Then most computers require lawful operational systems and can be used with extensive information technology connected to other devices such as cell phones, and amateur radio equipment as some activity can be considered Unconstitutional. Understanding these issues, there are hundreds of other internet, computer systems, television, and radio station companies that are active with good and bad technology, and therefore this resource of technology has taken off financially in a vast amount of good and sometimes bad ways.

As America is a capitalist society, it also means that groups of people, and various individuals will try or even pursue the dictatorship of other people in destructive ways. Understanding issues of a dictatorship most valued societies consist of a lack of opportunities and lawfully valued ways of advancement. Observing a society of logical advancement, fair business resources, and prosperity should not be distracted unlawfully. This means a capitalist society does not have to be full of dictators or evil people, but more so logical entrepreneurs, and investors as respectful hardworking people, and businesses that are working together to accomplish numerous industry standards, and valued goals.

# THE U.S. CONSTITUTION WITH AN ENDLESS LOOP CRISIS AND ANGER

(17)

## CHAPTER SEVENTEEN

(17)

Anger and Technology In America

Worse Than The Watergate Crisis, Without Domestic Tranquility

# THE U.S. CONSTITUTION WITH AN ENDLESS LOOP CRISIS AND ANGER

(17)

As the United States Constitution states; "We The People" -- this set of established laws are vital to all American people within all governed territorial states as lately an Endless Loop can and has been a critical problem, and crisis. Then these Constitutionally guided state and federally connected government's are valued with numerous amendments that have been challenged over the centuries and more so decades including now with "land and orbital satellite" technology. The best and most effective legal results can occur in various courts, individual state government Supreme Court's, and or the United States Supreme Court with expert professional or knowledgeable witnesses.

As the American society connects more satellites to personal computers, and numerous other devices we have approached the need to regulate this universal discipline, and format of mostly orbital satellite and computer technology. The resource of diversified satellites, computers, and the internet has created artificial intelligence that man or woman and the United States government is having a hard time controlling and or regulating. So we have recognized more bazaar anger apart from the Constitution's Domestic Tranquility. Therefore our history of technological studies and experiments have become like the Frankenstein monster invention with critically uncontrollable surprises of crucial madness that were not properly anticipated by Doctor Frankenstein, and the community of Transylvania.

The United States and Russia (c/o some German scientist & technology) began a race for outer- space, and to explore scientifically unknown planets, parts of the orbital universe, and then a man (astronaut - John Glenn) to visit and accomplish the 1968 walk on the Moon. Outer space exploration later in the years included the Chinese and more so Japanese government with orbital activities. Also this vitally included the advancements of satellite technology during the 1950s which began extensive earth (c/o land and water) exploration. Considering these U.S. government explorations, and advancements for years this was valuable research to American and worldwide scientist, engineers, businesses, other professionals and therefore various U.S. Constitutional law issues did not need to be adjusted or amended right away. Then space travel (c/o the United Nations) became like other inventions (cars & airplanes) as worldwide efforts began to consist of good, bad, and different national opinions, foreign relations, and other conflicting activities.

After Russia positioned Sputnik-1 into the orbit of outer-space, the United States government (c/o President's Dwight Eisenhower, and then John Kennedy) began lunching rockets into outer space with reconnaissance satellites. This also involved America with a few other clear understandings of various earthly issues in comparison to explore the orbital values of the Moon. Most of these scientist, engineers, and astronauts provided efforts which helped the United States government establish the National Aeronautics and Space Administration (NASA), and the National Oceanic and Atmospheric Administration (NOAA) as it exist today. Now as myself (JR's - Hurn Foundation), a few others like the Secured World Foundation and some U.S Defense Department concerns recognize America must defend its presents in outer space against other nations. Then I now also believe it's vitally important that we (the U.S.) must defend the American people (c/o innocence) from unlawful or destructive satellite technology which becomes more active between "orbital satellites connecting to computers on the planet Earth", and the United States.

Americas national studies and experiments of computer science, outer-space, various depths of the ocean, weather predictions, and communication systems are levels of effort which became issues of science and technology advancements, and sometimes evaluated fatal disasters. Then these are the good and bad issues of today's appropriate conditions of effective NASA, and NOAA duties and experimental issues of operations. This includes the good, bad, and complexity of rocketry, satellite programmed systems, computer programmed systems, and other important technology that must be evaluated. These are U.S. Constitutionally vital evaluations for logical "scientific principals and artificial intelligence" along with social standards throughout the American society. Observing enormous anger, these factors seem to be evidence of a tremendous and complex commercial airspace crisis throughout most regions of America which computers, satellites, and people interact.

Within the formal concept of a challenge along with the experiments of computers and satellites this includes device programming to create hopefully lawful industry and social standards. Then various Endless

Loop computer and satellite programming statements of operating systems became a critical need for liable and legal revisions from certain programming corrective responsible duties. As satellites are more advanced (c/o inadmissibility) and more so the unworkable conditions of an Endless Loop crisis, certain values of technology and laws have a vital need for revisions, corrections, and government oversight to secure the peoples long term existence. Otherwise this becomes valuable within the studies and resources of computer and satellite programming for extensive earth, orbit, and human interactions of artificial intelligence.

The extensive multitude of computers and satellites over the last 5 to 6 decades throughout the American society, and world still has Endless Loop, and legal concerns applicable to scientific-principals, Constitutional Amendments, and other laws. These concerns become national and international conflicts that must be corrected and lawfully workable as it applies to the American society for "Domestic Tranquility". Then the amended factor of numerous professional and social standards can consist of overall prosperous living.

As various constitutional amendments and technology must be lawfully workable, all types of people with the intervention of technology and laws must be aware of product liability or the disciplined use of powerful systems or dangerous products. Even our resource of nature (plants, animals, or humans) which all things must have potential to survive in prosperous ways is a vital necessity. Observing this fact, we as Americans and some foreign allies recognize this from various oil drilling and production spill concerns, nuclear testing, and the "Atom Bombs" America used on Hiroshima and Nagasaki in World War II. To this day even the U.S. government and some foreign allies have been slightly astonished about the amount of damage that these explosive bombs had caused.

The clear problem in the United States is the numerous violations of the Constitution's 1$^{st}$ Amendment, and the 4$^{th}$ Amendment along with other constitutional amendments and executive orders that apply to "logical confidentiality, free speech" and other personal human values. As tremendous as these issues are, and can become with people hearing voices in the commercial airspace, these issues can have an effect on hundreds, thousands, or millions of American people. This includes people's Constitutional rights which seem to be not just violated, but people having pretty much the misunderstanding of "No Constitutional Rights" to this Looping effect with anger which applies to various human resources of technology. Therefore this type of crisis is severe and can be more complex than most normal standards of technology that a majority of American citizens live by, and or recognize.

Considering technology standards, scientific-principals, and the Constitutional Rights in legal cases, this sometimes has consisted of judges and other government officials whom were occasionally violating those rights of the people before and after a plea agreement. Then this becomes not just an issue of "foreign or U.S. domestic spy's" and technology use issues within satellites or Constitutional law violations, but also government and some business officials causing a Lack Of Full Sovereignty for "We The People". Therefore the balance of hardworking people (c/o education and employment) is severely not helping some people exceed the poverty level, and this becomes a problem, and crisis as they don't prosper with domestic tranquility.

As the American society of government along with numerous public, private, small, large, and or corporate businesses exist -- numerous conflicts with "public, private business or government satellite bullies" can be a tremendous problem and crisis. This becomes vital to the victimization of people including the cause and issue of them to become suspects, and or defendants of an angry or misunderstood violent capacity. This is conditionally the issue of American concern that no domestic murder, or mass murder cases have made it to any part of a State, Federal, or the U.S. federal Supreme Court especially with the argument of Domestic Tranquility.

The concept of conviction within persons of these massive murders whom were considered by attorneys, certain experts, and or justice members includes concerns within the courts as it's valuable to say whether or not attorneys would take the case. Otherwise this becomes valuable for clear arguments to the local and highest courts as the overall society, industry, and financial determination for Constitutional justice has conflicts of discipline for the corrections of need. Therefore the corrective issue within Non-Domestic Tranquility or mental illness issues like these concerns argued in the case of Andrea Yates 2001 (5 children killed) of Texas, Kevin Isom 2007 (3 people killed) of Gary, Indiana, and a few others. These are two people as defendants that lived, and their case's reviewed many times throughout our court system of Justice, but satellite or other technology was not reviewed or determined as a factor.

If justice within the American system of courts and trail hearings are to help provide a solution to a problem or crisis, we still seem to have a way to go as it applies to massive anger, and even some technology. The constant

Loop of mass murders, domestic murder, and or suicide intensified during February of 2016 as there was at least 3 major violent acts -- one mass murder in Kalamazoo, Michigan, one mass murder in Wichita, Kansas, and one triple murder suicide in Merrillville, Indiana which means there was probably another somewhere else. As multiple people were killed and injured in these tragic acts it seems that conscious thinking and decision making by various people is complex as they are not able to always escape this Endless Loop of provoked anger. Therefore executive, legislative, and judicial evaluations of domestic tranquility, and artificial intelligence may be the best logic to improve enforcement.

Considering these mass murders in February 2016 between Kalamazoo and Wichita certain Endless Loop crisis technology connections were outlines in a Michigan court appearance along with a psychiatric evaluation. This was due to the metal behavior, and fatal violence of Jason Dalton shooting and killing 6 people in Kalamazoo, Michigan whiling driving for Uber Company which is an online transportation network company. He made statements that when the Uber (satellite & internet) screen in his vehicle went blank they were trying to make a puppet out of him. Therefore the concept of artificial intelligence has somewhat move into a courtroom setting which some issues should have been considered over 20 years ago. This was before Uber was created, and how this applied to numerous other violent conflicts. Theoretically in Kansas Cedric Ford (killed 3 & injured 14 other people) as the other shooter during February 2016, he was shot and killed by police so no testimony within complex evidence will come from him.

As communication systems will continue to advance, the 4th Amendment discusses affirmation which is a value to make sure that too many people don't try to be spy's, organizations do not live by disrespectful gossip on other Americans private matters, search warrants are lawfully outlined, and people obtaining information illegally are prosecuted or kept in order. These are issues similar to the Watergate scandal, and other issued tragedies which the valued loss of business, family values, financial values, or the insecurity of most logical resources of local and national government issues are maintained with resourceful duties. Detroit, Chicago, Jersey City, Gary, and various other cities and regions need to understand and have economic disciplines within the benefit of all these laws. Therefore the American society including government can become a positive factor of the changing times along with hopefully less anger or violence with safe and lawful overall technological standards.

# INDEX

Printed in the United States
By Bookmasters